THE
SHORTEST
HISTORY
OF
WAR

ALSO BY GWYNNE DYER

Growing Pains: The Future of Democracy (and Work)

Don't Panic! Isis, Terror and the
Making of the Middle East

Climate Wars

After Iraq

War

THE
SHORTEST
HISTORY
OF
WAR

**From Hunter-Gatherers to Nuclear
Superpowers—A Retelling for Our Times**

GWYNNE DYER

THE EXPERIMENT

NEW YORK

The Experiment, LLC
220 East 23rd Street, Suite 600
New York, NY 10010-4658
theexperimentpublishing.com

THE EXPERIMENT and its colophon are registered trademarks of The Experiment, LLC. Many of the designations used by manufacturers and sellers to distinguish their products are claimed as trademarks. Where those designations appear in this book and The Experiment was aware of a trademark claim, the designations have been capitalized.

The Experiment's books are available at special discounts when purchased in bulk for premiums and sales promotions as well as for fund-raising or educational use. For details, contact us at info@theexperimentpublishing.com.

Library of Congress Cataloging-in-Publication Data available upon request

ISBN 978-1-61519-930-3
Ebook ISBN 978-1-61519-931-0

Cover design by Jack Dunnington
Text design by Old Street Publishing, LTD
Illustrations by James Nunn

Manufactured in the United States of America

First printing August 2022
10 9 8 7 6 5 4 3 2 1

For Alice

Contents

Foreword

There is always another war to analyze, and I've done some of that in my time. But this is not that sort of book. It's about how war as a whole works, and why we do it, and even how we might stop. In many countries popular opinion has finally turned against war as a way of doing business, but almost every nation still keeps an army, however remote the possibility that they will have to use it may seem to most of them.

We have made significant progress. No great power has fought another directly in three quarters of a century, the longest interval in the past several thousand years. They may sometimes wage proxy wars or attack smaller, weaker countries, but their weapons have become so destructive that they have repeatedly avoided open war with each other, despite some terrifying crises.

Moreover, the toll of war in lives lost and cities destroyed has fallen steeply since 1945, when more than a million people were being killed each month. By the 1970s it was down to a million a year, and it is now in the low hundreds of thousands—fewer people than die in traffic accidents. Indeed, apart from the chronic conflict zones in southwestern Asia and Africa, as of this writing, there is only one war of any size underway anywhere in the world.

There are also international organizations and laws, almost all new since the Second World War, that aim to reduce the threat of war and restrict its impact on civilians, and they have had some successes. The media constantly feed us new images of war because they know we cannot resist watching them, but they usually come from the same few places. Despite occasional dramatic events like the war in Ukraine, this is probably the most peaceful time in world history.

Yet the weapons are still there, more lethal than ever before. The general staffs still make their plans, the armies still train their soldiers to kill (these days quite explicitly), and defense budgets have actually grown in most countries in the past ten years. Even in this time of unprecedented peace and prosperity, war continues to be seen as possible by both the soldiers and the diplomats. And harsher times are coming.

The bill is falling due on our two-century binge of eightfold population growth and mass industrialization, and we will find it very hard to pay. The climate is already moving out of the stable state in which we have grown our civilization over the past ten thousand years, and we will be lucky if we can stabilize it before it passes the +2°C threshold and goes runaway.

Even if we succeed in avoiding that calamity, the delayed action of greenhouse gas emissions already in the atmosphere but not yet producing their full effect on the climate, plus the effect of the other emissions that are bound to follow even if we now take the most radical steps to switch from fossil fuels to other sources of energy, will cause enough warming to do great damage to global food production, particularly in the tropics and sub-tropics.

That will almost certainly lead to refugee flows far larger than anything we have seen in the past, forcing governments in the destination countries to make agonizing choices about whom to let in and whom to keep out—and what means can legitimately be used to keep them out. Governments that cannot feed their people tend not to survive, so we may end up with large "ungoverned" spaces in some of the worst affected countries—think ten to twenty Somalias. Countries that share major river systems may find it hard to avoid war when the total flow is way down and the upstream country is tempted to keep more of the remaining water for its own people.

These future probabilities, not often discussed in public, are already being taken into account in the strategic assessments that are made by senior planning staffs in the largest military powers. It's not that they are looking for trouble, but it is their professional responsibility to foresee and prepare for it. In their judgment, there is big trouble coming that cannot be, or at least probably will not be dealt with by nonmilitary means. War between the great powers, the kind of war that kills in the millions, is not dead. It's only sleeping, and recently it has been twitching a bit.

This is bad news, but it is also a good reason to reexamine the whole phenomenon of war. Until only a century ago—up to midway through the First World War, say—the general view was that war is a noble enterprise and a Good Thing (provided you win). The mass slaughter of citizen-soldiers in the trenches put an end to that, and ever since, the attentive public has believed, correctly, that war is a Problem. They didn't even have to wait for nuclear weapons to come to that conclusion.

Most of us, though, are not very well informed about where war comes from or how it really works. This is in large part because we fear that too close an examination will undermine the reverence and gratitude we feel toward those who sacrificed their lives in our own country's wars. Nevertheless, with due respect for the "fallen" (and they deserve better than such a weasel word), we should proceed.

This is not a military history in the usual sense, although I trained as a military historian and spent the first half of my adult life kicking around various parts of the military. It is a study of war as a custom and tradition, as a political and social institution, and as a Problem.

Tactics, strategy, doctrine, and technology will figure prominently, as cutting people open would in a history of surgery, but they are not the prime focus. The human beings who must accept the extraordinary demands of this institution, leaders and ordinary soldiers alike, must be part of the story too. Mostly, though, it's a book about why we do this thing, and how we might stop doing it, now that we really need to.

CHAPTER 1

Origins

How Old Is War?

Human beings did not invent war. They inherited it. Our most distant ancestors practiced it, as do some of our primate near-relatives down to this day. Yet for the past couple of centuries most people have believed that war grew with civilization, and had not been a major problem for our hunter-gatherer predecessors.

This belief was strongly promoted in the mid-eighteenth century by Jean-Jacques Rousseau, one of the most influential philosophers of the Enlightenment, who argued that the "noble savages" who had lived before the rise of the mass civilizations had lived in freedom and equality—and, he implied, also in peace. We could recover that lost paradise if only we got rid of the kings and the priests who currently oppressed the civilized lands. It was an attractive idea, and in his own time people were beginning to act on it. He died two years after the outbreak of the American Revolution, and only eleven years before the far greater upheaval of the French Revolution.

Rousseau would have known that the "noble savages" of his own time did occasionally fight each other, but their armed clashes were small, caused few casualties, and seemed a world away from the terrible battles between the great armies of civilization. Even two centuries later, when anthropologists began to study the few hunter-gatherer groups that had survived into the modern world, they continued to see the occasional armed conflicts between these little bands—as few as thirty people, and almost always fewer than a hundred—as essentially ritual activities with a low cost in lives. It's only in the past fifty years that we have realized how wrong they were.

You can't blame Rousseau for getting it wrong. In his time knowledge of the past only went back around three thousand years. Nobody knew how old the Earth was (4.5 billion years), or anything about evolution (our own hominin lineage diverged from that of the chimpanzees between 4 and 5.5 million years ago), or even when *Homo sapiens* first appeared (c. 300,000 years ago). It's harder to understand how anthropologists managed to ignore for so long the evidence that was piling up on their doorstep, but they went on believing Rousseau until quite late in the twentieth century.

They ignored the narrative evidence of people like William Buckley, who escaped from a penal colony on the south coast of Australia in 1803 and lived for thirty-two years as a fugitive among the Aborigines.

> On the hostile tribe coming near, I saw they were all men . . .
> In a very short time the fight began . . . [Two members of Buckley's band were killed in the clash, but they counter-attacked that night] and finding most of them asleep and laying about in groups, our party rushed upon them, killing three on the spot, and wounding several others . . . The enemy fled . . . leaving their war implements in the hands of their assailants and their wounded to be beaten to death by boomerangs.[1]

They ignored equally the work of pioneer ethnologist Lloyd Warner, who studied the Murngin people of Arnhem Land in northern Australia in the early twentieth century. The Murngin had only recently come into regular contact with Europeans and their oral history tradition was still strong, so people actually knew and could relate the deeds done by and to their grandparents and great grandparents. Through extensive interviews Warner tried to reconstruct the scale of warfare among local aboriginal bands in the late nineteenth century (before first contact). He concluded that the chronic low-level raiding and ambushes, rarely killing more than one or two people at a time, nevertheless accounted over the twenty-year period he studied for the deaths of about 25 percent of the adult males in the various bands that made up the Murngin people (population c. 3,000).[2] But Warner was largely overlooked by the budding profession of anthropology: Rousseau still reigned.

Fierce People

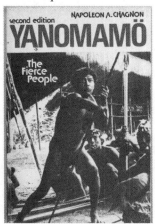

Fierce Reaction: Chagnon's
controversial study

The debate finally opened up with the publication in 1968 of *Yanomamo: The Fierce People*, anthropologist Napoleon Chagnon's study of the Yanomamo people living in southern Venezuela and northern Brazil on the headwaters of the Orinoco and Amazon Rivers. The Yanomamo were some twenty-five thousand people divided among about 250 villages that were constantly at war with one another. Technically they were not hunter-gatherers but "horticulturalists," practicing a form of slash-and-burn agriculture that required them to move their villages every few years. But their group size was about the same (an average of ninety people per village), and so were their social customs, including the custom of warfare.

Their villages were fortified, and there were huge buffer zones between them—up to thirty miles in some cases, presumably because raiding parties can travel far and fast. Moreover, the Yanomamo tended to stay in the central parts of their territory, venturing into the border zones only in large groups and leaving them mostly unexploited. From time to time entire villages would be destroyed. And the average death toll of this chronic warfare over a generation, Chagnon calculated, was 24 percent of the men and 7 percent of the women.[3]

Chagnon's ideas gained some traction, and his book became a staple of the university curriculum. But the notion of an in-built tendency to war was just too much of an affront to the doctrines of Rousseau, and to those anthropologists who tended his flame. A backlash from the old guard saw Chagnon accused of distorting or even fabricating his data, and for a time the Venezuelan government banned him from going back to visit the Yanomamo. It was 2012, seven years before Chagnon's death, before he was rehabilitated sufficiently to gain admission to the US National Academy of Sciences.

Anthropologist Ernest Burch had an easier time. In the 1960s he conducted a similar investigation into hunter-gatherer warfare among the Inuit of northwestern Alaska. The warfare had largely ended after contact was established with Europeans and Americans about ninety years before, but drawing on historical records and the memories of old men, he concluded that there used to be at least one war a year in the region: between Inuit bands in the local area; against other Inuit from farther away; even against Athabasca First Nation groups in what is now the Yukon. Alliances were constantly shifting as rival groups tried to attain numerical superiority, and the ultimate goal of the war was generally the annihilation of the opposing group.

The Inuit warriors wore body armor made of bone or ivory fragments strung together like chain mail under their outer garments, and raiding parties as big as fifty men would travel for many days to attack their enemies. From time to time there were set-piece battles in which lines of men would face each other, but more often there were predawn raids on sleeping villages, which would sometimes end in wholesale massacres. Male warriors were not taken prisoner unless they were to be kept for later torture and killing, and women and children were not normally spared. A decade earlier his data would have ignited a huge controversy, but Burch did not publish his conclusions until 1974, and by that time the cat was out of the bag.[4]

Chimp Wars

Curiously, the final nail in Rousseau's coffin was not another anthropological study, but came from the primatologist Jane Goodall. While observing a chimpanzee troop in Gombe National Park in Tanzania, Goodall noted that her troop also waged war against the neighboring band. Since human beings share more than 99 percent of their DNA with chimpanzees,

Lady and the Chimp: Jane Goodall with David Greybeard, c. 1965

and have constantly waged war almost everywhere at least since the hunter-gatherer stage, it seems probable that this behavior is shared by the hominin and chimp lineages all the way back to our last common ancestor over four million years ago.

The chimpanzee clashes were even more distant from civilized warfare than the "wars" of human hunter-gatherers. Chimpanzees rarely use weapons (the occasional tree branch, perhaps), and it is not easy for one chimpanzee to kill another with his bare hands. There are never pitched battles between chimpanzee bands; all the killing is done by ambush, in which a number of chimpanzees from one band encounter an isolated individual from a rival band.

> It began as a border patrol. At one point . . . they spotted Goliath [an elderly chimp], apparently hiding only twenty-five meters away. The raiders rushed madly down the slope to their target. While Goliath screamed and the troop hooted and displayed, he was held and beaten and kicked and lifted and dropped and bitten and jumped on . . . They kept up the attack for eighteen minutes, then turned for home . . . Bleeding freely from his head, gashed on his back, Goliath tried to sit up but fell back shivering. He too was never seen again.
>
> Richard Wrangham and Dale Peterson, *Demonic Males: Apes and the Origins of Human Violence*[5]

Was it really war? Well, these attacks did not happen every time a patrol caught a lone member from a rival band. They would listen for the calls that other members of the rival group made to keep in touch as they moved through the forest, and only attacked if there were no members of that band nearby who might come to the aid of the intended victim. Otherwise, they would quietly withdraw and leave it for another day. But it was deadly serious stuff. Despite their extreme caution and the fact that the killing was always done one chimp at a time, there were instances when all the males of one troop were finally eliminated. Thereupon the males of the rival band would move in, appropriate the surviving females, and kill the existing babies to make room for their own.

Some of these chimpanzee bands have been observed for fifty years now, and across all the bands studied, this endemic warfare ultimately caused the deaths of about 30 percent of the adult males and 5 percent of the females. The territories controlled by the chimpanzee bands were far smaller than those of Yanomamo villages—only three or four miles between one band and the next—but the chimps spent almost all their time in the central third of their territory. The rest of the territory was equally rich in resources, but was treated as a "no-man's-land" and only visited in large groups due to the danger of ambush and death at the hands of a neighboring troop.[6]

Murngin hunter-gatherers in Arnhem Land, Yanomamo horticulturalists in Amazonia, chimpanzees in Gombe: a bell was tolling for our illusions in the way these statistics lined up. They signaled a style of warfare whose casualties were proportionally far greater than anything experienced by modern civilizations, and that was very ancient indeed. Archaeologists were alerted to start looking for evidence of warfare in the fossil record of humans and closely related species. It wasn't long before they found it.

They found *Homo erectus* fossils from 750,000 years ago bearing signs of violence inflicted by human-style weapons, like depression fractures in skulls (perhaps made by clubs) and cut-marks on bones that suggest de-fleshing and cannibalism. Such killings generally require complex purification rituals afterward, and ritual cannibalism is often part of them. They also found Neanderthal fossils dating back to between forty thousand and a hundred thousand years ago with injuries inflicted by spears, a stone blade lodged between the ribs, even mass graves.[7]

Going forward to just a few thousand years before the rise of the first civilizations, they found scenes of mass slaughter that could only have been associated with war, like the twenty-seven people massacred at Nataruk, west of Lake Turkana in Kenya, about ten thousand years ago. They were men, women, and children, mostly clubbed or stabbed to death (although six were probably killed by arrows), and their bodies were not buried but left to rot. The media treated it as a revelation, but no doubt it was just another incident among tens or hundreds of thousands of similar ones in the long prehistory of human and hominid warfare. So what are we to make of all this?

Two Conditions

Do we bear the mark of Cain? Are we simply doomed to wage ever greater wars until we finally destroy ourselves? Not necessarily. But we do meet the two conditions needed to account for the warlike behavior of any species toward other members of its own kind: Is the species predatory, and does it live in *groups of variable size*?

We and our ancestors have been hunters for millions of years, and we can therefore easily kill other human beings. Indeed, we have been able to kill even the largest animals for at least a couple hundred thousand years, so we definitely tick the "predator" box. (Chimpanzees, who regularly hunt, catch, and eat monkeys and other small game, are the only other primate species to tick that box—and also the only other primate species that fights wars.)

On the face of it, "living in groups of variable size" is a more puzzling requirement, but it works like this. Solitary predators rarely engage in serious fights with other members of the same species, because there's about a 50 percent chance of death in such an encounter, and it's just not worth it in evolutionary terms. In any case, warfare is by definition a group activity. But if those groups are all of similar size, and their members stick together, the likelihood of a head-on battle is equally low: they would be more or less evenly matched, there would be lots of deaths, and any victory would be pyrrhic.

By contrast, groups of variable size, which must sometimes split up into smaller groups or single individuals to forage, present opportunities for ambushes in which the odds will be very much in favor of the attackers. Attritional warfare is thus possible between such groups, and although the attacks are mostly opportunistic, they may result in the extermination of all the males in one of the groups. Lions behave like this, and wolves and hyenas too, and of course chimps and humans—all predators that live in groups of variable size. But what benefit are the winning groups actually getting out of this? What evolutionary advantage does it confer?

The world was never empty, and food has always been limited. Whether the environment is desert, jungle, seashore, or savanna, both the predator and the prey species will tend to breed up to the carrying capacity of the environment—and a bit beyond it. Human hunter-gatherers often practiced infanticide as a form of birth control, but the decision to expose the infant seems generally to have been taken by overburdened parents, not imposed as a matter of band policy. It probably didn't slow population growth very much.

If your band is living up around the maximum carrying capacity of the local environment, even a brief interruption in food supply (e.g., changes in the weather pattern or in animal migration routes) will create an instant crisis, since most of the foods people eat cannot be stored. In a matter of weeks or months everybody is hungry all the time, and since human beings are gifted with foresight, they know what lies ahead for most of the group if this goes on. But if your band has been systematically culling the adult male population of the neighboring band by serial ambushes for a long time, it may now have the option of going for broke, exterminating the rest of the neighboring band's males, and taking over their food resources to get you through the crisis.

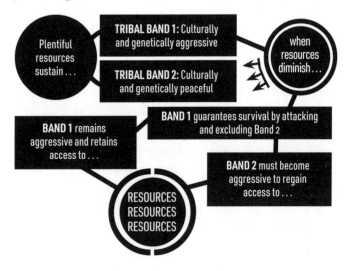

Plentiful resources sustain . . .

TRIBAL BAND 1: Culturally and genetically aggressive

TRIBAL BAND 2: Culturally and genetically peaceful

when resources diminish . . .

BAND 1 remains aggressive and retains access to . . .

BAND 1 guarantees survival by attacking and excluding Band 2

BAND 2 must become aggressive to regain access to . . .

RESOURCES RESOURCES RESOURCES

Evolution is not driven by rational calculation, and the chronic warfare that fills our prehistory was not consciously designed as a device for ensuring the survival of our own genetic line. But to explain it, you only have to assume that there was always some degree of competition for resources between neighboring bands, even in good times, and that in bad times some groups might be driven to violence. Whether for cultural or genetic reasons, some bands will be at least marginally more aggressive than others. Those are the bands that are likeliest to survive when the resources get scarce, and to pass on both their culture and their genes to the next generation. Put these factors on a low heat and stir occasionally for a few hundred generations, and you get the plight of the Yanomamo people.

> [Yanomamo] villages are situated in the forest among neighboring villages they do not, and cannot, fully trust. Most of the Yanomamo people regard their perpetual inter-village warfare as dangerous and ultimately reprehensible, and if there were a magic way to end it perfectly and certainly, undoubtedly they would choose that magic. But they know there is no such thing. They know that their neighbors are, or can soon turn into, the bad guys: treacherous and committed enemies. In the absence of full trust, Yanomamo villages deal with one another through trading, inter-marriage, the formal creation of imperfect political treaties—and by inspiring terror through an implacable readiness for revenge.
>
> Wrangham and Peterson, *op. cit.*, 65[8]

Just change the names around, and this would serve as an explanation of the relationship between the great powers in the period before the outbreak of the First World War in 1914. And just as the trigger for the First World War—the assassination of an Austrian archduke in a Balkan town—seemed a trivial cause for such a huge event, so the explanations the Yanomamo gave for their wars seem pathetic and even ridiculous. In fact, they usually blamed them on conflicts over women. But many people always suspected that there was something deeper going on too.

Equality and War
So far, Rousseau has been a full-spectrum failure as an armchair anthropologist, but he did get one thing right. It was a very

big thing: he said that pre-civilized human beings, his "noble savages," had lived in complete freedom and absolute equality. In fact, this was the main reason for his great popularity: he was finding a precedent in the past for people who wanted to make revolutions in the present—revolutions that would make people free and equal *again*. He was guessing, but it was a very good guess.

> All men seek to rule, but if they cannot rule they prefer to remain equal.
> Harold Schneider, economic anthropologist[9]

> The three African great apes, with whom we share the relatively recent Common Ancestor, are notably hierarchical . . . but before twelve thousand years ago, humans basically were egalitarian.
> Bruce Knauft, cultural anthropologist[10]

For those who concern themselves with the nature of human nature, the greatest puzzle is the fact that all the hunter-gatherer societies and almost all the horticultural societies we know of were egalitarian, at least when it came to adult males. Not just a little bit egalitarian, but intensely, even obsessively so, and this cultural preference continues to be visible even in their descendants who have long had contact with the mass societies of civilization. The elders may carry authority in debate, the top hunters may get the best parts of the kill, but no single individual has the power of command.

This is a puzzle because the empires, absolute monarchies, and dictatorships that fill our written history until quite recently were extremely hierarchical, unequal, oppressive societies. So are the little societies of our nearest primate relatives, the other great apes, and in particular the chimpanzees who are the closest of all. Chimpanzee bands are tyrannies in which the dominant male enforces his rule by dramatic displays of rage frequently accompanied by physical attacks on the other band members, to which they generally respond with gestures of submission.

Living out your life in a little band ruled by a bad-tempered despot is not much fun. There are constant attempts by the subordinate males, who can only have sex with the females in the band when out of the boss's sight, to put together coalitions that will overthrow the dominant male. Sooner or later one of these conspiracies succeeds, generally when the top male is losing his ability to frighten all the others into submission because of age or injury. Unfortunately for the chimps, this only produces a new boss who behaves much like the old one. You would not choose to be born a chimpanzee.

We cannot know when a different system of values became dominant among human beings, but it must have been a very long time ago, probably many tens of thousands of years, because egalitarian values and the social attitudes and customs that support them are the norm in almost every aboriginal culture we know of, from the Arctic to the tropics, in deserts or forests, on every continent.

> By my definition, egalitarian society is the product of a large, well-united coalition of subordinates who assertively deny political power to the would-be alphas in their group.
> Christopher Boehm, evolutionary anthropologist[11]

Humans were different from the other great apes in two key respects: they were more intelligent, and they had language. The intelligence allowed them to figure out that their personal chances of emerging as "top dog" in the constant struggle for power were not very good. Ending up toward the bottom of the pecking order, spending their lives being bullied and beaten, undesirable as that might be, was much more likely. It was a relatively short step from there to realizing that the solution would be to overthrow the boss and enforce equality among all the adult males.

A bright chimpanzee might dimly grasp this concept, but he would have no language in which to express it clearly even to himself, let alone to the other chimps who might join a successful conspiracy. Humans did have language, and could put together a coalition that would not only overthrow the existing despot but shut the whole dominance game down permanently. Obviously, they did just that. Not only once, but thousands of times in thousands of different bands, because the example would spread rapidly.

It was Christopher Boehm who first articulated this notion, which he calls a "reverse dominance hierarchy." His model does not require us to reinvent human beings as a species without ambition or envy in order to explain what happened. All it needs is a coalition of subordinate males to use their superior numbers to deter the alpha males from taking control. It rarely even requires physical force. As a !Kung hunter in the Kalahari Desert said to anthropologist Richard Lee, explaining how the social controls work:

> When a young man kills much meat, he comes to think of himself as a chief or a big man, and he thinks of the rest of us as his servants or inferiors. We can't accept this . . . so we always speak of his meat as worthless. In this way we cool his heart and make him gentle.[12]

Every hunter-gatherer band that anthropologists have had an opportunity to study was fiercely egalitarian. The greatest social crime was for one adult male to give an order to another. Decisions were made, when they were needed, by a process of discussion that could last for days, leading to a consensus that was still not binding. People married outside the group, so if you truly hated the decision you could always leave and join another band where you had relatives.

In aboriginal groups with relatively intact cultures, the tall poppies are always cut down, at least metaphorically. The penalties for trying to put yourself above the others start with mockery and move up through ostracism to exile—or in the past, in extreme cases, even execution. The hunter-gatherers of the long past were not sweet, gentle stewards of nature; they were heavily armed men, proficient in violence, who fought frequent wars with neighboring bands, for the egalitarian revolution did not eliminate the wars. They would kill if necessary to "defend the revolution" (as they certainly would not have put it), but once "reverse dominance" was firmly established, they may not have had to do that very often.

When did this revolution happen? Not before a hundred thousand years ago, because if human beings had already had enough language for that kind of sophisticated plotting before the last interglacial warm period (131,000–114,000 years ago), they would probably have started in on agriculture, mass civilization, and all the rest way back then. They certainly didn't waste any time in getting started once the current interglacial arrived. It's unlikely to have been less than twenty thousand years ago, because entrenching the egalitarian values so deeply in human cultures (and maybe even in the human genome) that those values would survive millennia of universal tyranny unchanged would have taken a long time. But we cannot be more precise.

A Bushman family, 2017

One remarkable by-product of this great change was the institution of the human family. In a band where all the adult males were equal, a single dominant male was no longer trying to monopolize sexual access to the females of the band in the usual primate way. (Was this part of the motivation for the revolution? Probably yes.) Gender equality was not part of the revolution, but henceforth each free and equal male would likely end up with one female consort in a more or less stable relationship, and would know, or at least think he knew, which children were his. He might even help to raise them.

The Great Change

And so we arrived at the brink of the agricultural revolution ten thousand years ago, a species transformed. We had colonized every habitable part of the Earth apart from a few ocean islands like Madagascar and New Zealand, and we probably numbered around four million people, all still living in those little ancestral bands. War took a constant toll on all of those bands (except perhaps a few who lived in splendid isolation), but those who stayed alive were free, healthy for the most part, and maybe even happy. Then we became farmers, and everything changed.

Well, not quite everything. War remained.

CHAPTER 2

How Combat Works

The Province of Uncertainty

A lone US Marine in Vietnam (1966)

This is a history, so it will spend a lot of time in the past. But the past is a continuum that slides seamlessly into the present, and any attempt at Big History (even a very short one) is at least in part an attempt to understand the here and now. It is useful, therefore, to recall how war actually works in the present—the last hundred years, say—before plunging back into the past. Never mind the strategy or the technology for the moment; just concentrate on the experience of the people who do the fighting on the ground.

War is the province of uncertainty; three-fourths of the things on which action in war is based lie hidden in the fog of greater or lesser uncertainty.

Karl von Clausewitz

As we were going into the position, there was a large rice field we had to walk across, and I remember that I had to send somebody else across first. Now there was one moment of hesitation, when he looked at me: "Do you mean me? Do you really mean it?" And the look I must have given him— he knew that I meant it, and he went across the field.

I started sending them across in twos, and it was no problem. Then I took my entire force across. When we were about halfway across, they came up behind us, the VC [Viet Cong], and they were in spiderholes, and they caught most of my unit in the open.

Now tactically I had done everything the way it was supposed to be done, but we lost some soldiers. So did I make a mistake? I don't know. Would I have done it differently [another time]? I don't think I would have, because that's the way I was trained. Did we lose less soldiers by my doing it that way? That's a question that'll never be answered.

Maj. Robert Ooley, US Army

There is no good answer. In combat, officers have to make their decisions fast, without adequate information, while people (whom they generally cannot see) are trying to kill them. Those who get it wrong often die—and so do some of those who get it right. The best they can do is to cling to the rules that previous generations of officers have distilled from practical experience, even though they know that those rules are no guarantee of success. At best, they shift the odds a bit in your favor.

Major Ooley was trained in battle drills that aimed to reduce the risk of an unpleasant surprise, and limit the damage done if it happened anyway. Tactical doctrines are indispensable but never reliable, because there is no certainty about where the enemy is and what he is doing. Ooley fought a long, losing war in Vietnam, but even in short, victorious wars like the ones fought by General Yossi Ben-Chanaan, bad outcomes can't be avoided altogether.

During the 1973 Arab-Israeli War, Ben-Chanaan commanded an Israeli tank brigade on the Golan Heights. On the sixth day of the war, with only eight tanks left, he managed to get behind the Syrian front line.

> ... once we arrived to the rear we took position, and all their positions were very exposed. We opened fire, and for about twenty minutes we destroyed whoever we could see, because we were in a great position there.
>
> I decided to charge and try to get that hill, but I had to leave a couple of tanks in cover; so I charged with six tanks. [The Syrians] opened fire from the flank with anti-tank missiles, and in a matter of seconds, three out of the six tanks were blown up. There was a big explosion in my tank. I blew out, and I was left there ... And also the whole attack was a mistake, I think.

General Ben-Chanaan, as the commander, was riding head and shoulders out of the turret to see the situation better. It's a lethally exposed position if you come under machine-gun or artillery fire, but it's the best place to be if an anti-tank missile penetrates the hull. Ben-Chanaan was blown out of the turret; his crew down in the body of the tank was incinerated. He was a competent officer, but his attack failed and some of his men died. Commanders almost always have to accept a certain level of risk, because things are moving fast and they cannot afford to wait for better information.

The armed forces, with their uniforms, their rigid system of ranks, and their general intolerance for deviations from the norm, may seem overorganized and inflexible in peacetime, but peace is not their true working environment. In battle, the seeming absurdity of commands given and acknowledged in stilted terms, of absolute obedience to the most senior person present, of obliging every officer to report his situation in *this* format rather than some other (when there is no obvious advantage in doing it one way rather than another) are all useful because they reduce the unpredictability of an essentially chaotic situation.

Rank Necessity

Even the most bizarre aspect of military organization, the distinction between officers—who make the decisions—and the rank and file—who have to carry them out—makes sense in this peculiar situation. All military organizations are divided into two entirely separate hierarchies of people covering roughly the same span of age and often, at the junior levels, doing much the same kind of job. Army officers at the age of twenty are placed in charge of enlisted men who are older and more experienced than themselves. Indeed, the twenty-year-old second lieutenant, fresh from a year of officer cadet training, is legally of higher rank than the most senior NCO in the army, a regimental sergeant-major who will typically have served at least eighteen years before attaining that rank—and all armies make it very difficult to transfer from the enlisted ranks to the officer caste.

The officer/enlisted ranks distinction has its roots in the political and social structures of a distant past when nobles commanded and commoners obeyed, but even radically egalitarian states like revolutionary France or Bolshevik Russia never abolished it. It had to be preserved, because it is the duty of officers to expend their soldiers' lives in order to accomplish the purposes of the state.

> You've got to keep distant from [your soldiers]. The officer-enlisted man distance helps. This is one of the most painful things, having to withhold sometimes your affection for them, because you know you're going to have to destroy them on occasion. And you do. You use them up: they're material. And part of being a good officer is knowing how much of them you can use up and still get the job done.
>
> Paul Fussell, infantry officer, World War II

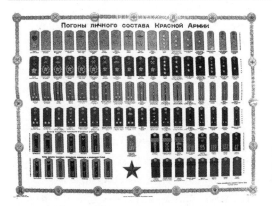

Red Army shoulder marks, c. 1943

Officers are *managers* of violence: except in the most extreme circumstances, they do not use weapons themselves. Their job is to direct those who do and make them go on doing it even unto death. This does not mean they do not care for their men, and it certainly does not mean that they are avoiding danger themselves. Indeed, officer casualties are usually higher proportionally than those of the enlisted men, mainly because they must expose themselves more in order to motivate their soldiers. In British and American infantry battalions in World War II, the proportion of officers who became casualties was around twice as high as the casualties among enlisted men. Similar figures apply for most other armies that have seen major combat in the past two centuries.[1]

> It occurred to me to count the number of officers who had served in the Battalion since D-Day. Up to March 27th, the end of the Rhine crossing [less than ten months] ... I found that we had had 55 officers commanding the twelve rifle platoons, and that their average service with the Battalion was 38 days ... Of these 53% were wounded, 24% killed or died of wounds, 15% invalided, and 5% survived.
>
> Col. M. Lindsay, 1st Gordon Highlanders[2]

The peculiar role that officers must play also gives them a special perspective on how the world works.

Professional Ethics

> The military ethic emphasises the permanence of irrationality, weakness and evil in human affairs. It stresses the supremacy of society over the individual and the importance of order, hierarchy and division of function.
>
> It accepts the nation state as the highest form of political organization and recognises the continuing likelihood of war among nation states ... It exalts obedience as the highest virtue of military men ... It is, in brief, realistic and conservative.
>
> Samuel Huntington[3]

Much of Huntington's classic definition of the "military mind" would have applied even in the distant past, but military officers have now become a separate and specialized profession.

Are they really a profession in the same sense as the medical and legal professions? In most respects, yes. The officer corps is a self-regulating body of specialists who choose who may join it and even who gets promoted (except at the highest levels where political considerations often predominate). The military profession is the monopoly supplier of the service it provides, and it enjoys some special privileges (like early retirement) because that service makes special demands on its members. Like doctors or lawyers, military officers also have a wide range of corporate interests to defend and advance. But there is one big difference: what soldiers call the "unlimited liability" of their contract to serve. Few other contracts oblige the employee to lay down his life when the employer demands it.

Politicians may . . . pretend that the soldier is ethically in no different position than any other professional. He is. He serves under an unlimited liability, and it is the unlimited liability which lends dignity to the military profession . . . There's also the fact that military action is group action, particularly in armies . . . The success of armies depends to a very high degree on the coherence of the group, and the coherence of the group depends on the degree of trust and confidence of its members in each other.

What Arnold Toynbee used to call the military virtues— fortitude, endurance, loyalty, courage, and so on—these are good qualities in any collection of men. But in the military society they are functional necessities, which is something quite, quite different. I mean, a man can be false, fleeting, perjured, in every way corrupt, and still be a brilliant mathematician or one of the world's greatest painters. But there's one thing he can't be, and that's a good soldier, sailor or airman.

Gen. Sir John Hackett

There are bad officers, of course, but the lack of those "military virtues" is what makes them bad officers. Those who have

Korean War. One infantryman comforts another while a third fills out body tags, August 25, 1950.

lived among military officers for any length of time will know that, while diverse in other respects, they are an uncommonly truthful and loyal group of people. Nor is this distinction confined to the officer corps: Stephen Bagnall, who served as a private with the 5th East Lancashires in Normandy in 1944, wrote in his memoir of the state of grace amid evil that prevails, by necessity, among frontline soldiers; of "the friendly helpfulness and almost gaiety that increases until it is an almost unbelievably tangible and incongruous thing as you get nearer to the front. A cousin writing to me recently . . . said, 'Men are never so loving or so lovable as they are in action.' That is not only true, it is the beginning and end of the matter."[4]

But it is not the whole of the truth.

Managing Breakdown

> I went where I was told to go and did what I was told to do, but no more. I was scared shitless just about all the time.
>
> James Jones, US infantry private, World War II

> If blood was brown, we'd all have medals.
>
> Canadian sergeant, northwest Europe, 1944–45

During World War II, the US Army used questionnaires to find out how affected its soldiers were by fear on the battlefield. In one infantry division in France in August 1944, two thirds of the soldiers admitted that they had not been able to do their jobs properly because of extreme fear at least once, and over two fifths said it had happened repeatedly.

In another infantry division in the South Pacific, over two thousand soldiers were asked about the physical symptoms of fear: 84 percent said they had a violent pounding of the heart, and over three fifths said they shook or trembled all over. Around half admitted to feeling faint, breaking out in a cold sweat, and feeling sick to their stomachs. Over a quarter said they had vomited, and 21 percent said they had lost control of their bowels.[5] These figures are based only on voluntary admissions, and the true percentages are probably higher in all categories, especially the more embarrassing ones. James Jones's remark about being "scared shitless" was not just a colorful expression.

This is the reality with which officers must contend in combat: soldiers whose training and pride, and even their loyalty to their close friends around them, are finely balanced against physical terror and a desperate desire not to die. They can turn into a panic-stricken mob if that balance tilts just a bit, so their officers must work very hard to keep them in action. In major wars of recent times, almost everybody falls apart eventually; the trick is to keep them from all doing it at the same time.

The dead and wounded in a major pre-twentieth-century battle often amounted to 40 or 50 percent of the men engaged. It was rarely less than 20 percent. Given a couple of battles a year, the infantryman therefore stood an even chance of being killed or wounded for each year the war continued—a very discouraging prospect. But the battles each lasted only one day, and for the other 363 days of the year the soldiers were usually not even in close contact with the enemy. They might be cold, wet, tired, and hungry much of the time, but for half the year they probably got to sleep indoors. The likelihood that they would be dead or wounded within the year could be dealt with in the same way other people deal with the eventual certainty of death: ignore it. Things are very different now.

> There is no such thing as "getting used to combat." Each moment of combat imposes a strain so great that men will break down in direct relation to the intensity and duration of their exposure.
>
> US Army investigation into the psychological effects of combat[6]

The casualty toll in a single day of battle has plummeted since the nineteenth century: the average daily loss for a division-sized force in intensive combat in World War II was about 2 percent of its personnel. The problem is that battles can now continue for weeks—and the battles follow each other in quick succession.

The cumulative loss rate is about the same as before, with infantrymen facing an even chance of death or a serious wound within a year, but the psychological impact of combat is very different. Troops are shelled every day, the enemy is always close, and they live amid constant death. This inexorably erodes men's faith in their own survival, and eventually destroys everybody's courage and will. "Your courage flows at its outset with the fullest force and thereafter diminishes; perhaps if you are very brave it diminishes imperceptibly, but it does diminish . . . and it can never behave otherwise," as Stephen Bagnall wrote.[7]

The US Army concluded during World War II that almost every soldier, if he escaped death or wounds, would break down after 200 to 240 "combat days." The British, who rotated their troops out of the front line more often, reckoned 400 days, but agreed that breakdown was inevitable. Only about one sixth of casualties were psychiatric, but that was because most combat troops did not survive long enough to go to pieces.

The trajectory of combat infantrymen was the same in every army. In the first few days of combat, they would experience constant fear and apprehension (though they would try to hide it). Once they had learned to distinguish the truly dangerous phenomena of combat from the merely frightening, their confidence and performance would steadily improve. After three weeks they would be at their peak—and then the long slide would begin.

By the sixth week of continuous combat, reported two army psychiatrists who accompanied a US infantry battalion in 1944, most soldiers had become convinced of the inevitability of their own death and had stopped believing that their skill or courage made any difference. They would go on functioning with gradually declining effectiveness for some months, but in the end, if they were not killed, wounded, or withdrawn from battle, the result was the same.

> As far as they were concerned the situation was one of absolute hopelessness . . . Mental defects became so extreme that [the soldier] could not be counted on to relay a verbal order . . . He remained almost constantly in or near his slit trench, and during acute actions took little or no part, trembling constantly.
>
> S. Bagnall, *The Attack* (1947)

At this point the "two-thousand-year stare" appeared. The next stage was catatonia or total disorientation and breakdown.[8]

Yet relatively few units collapsed, because there was a constant flow of replacements to replace the casualties (including those suffering from "combat fatigue"). Most units in prolonged combat in modern war, therefore, are an uneasy mixture of some green and unsure replacements, some veterans (many of whom are nearing breakdown), and a large group of soldiers—the bigger the better, from the unit's point of view—who are still in transition from "green" to burned out.

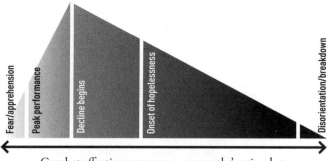

Combat effectiveness over 9–12 months' active duty

These are the people whom an officer must "use up" to get the job done. Their state of mind was eloquently described by US Army Brig. Gen. S. L. A. Marshall, a veteran of World War I and a historian of World War II and the Korean War.

> Wherever one surveys the forces of the battlefield, it is to see that fear is general among men, but to observe further that men commonly are loath that their fear will be expressed in specific acts which their comrades will recognize as cowardice. The majority are unwilling to take extraordinary risks and do not aspire to a hero's role, but they are equally unwilling that they should be considered the least worthy among those present . . .

> The seeds of panic are always present in troops so long as they are in the midst of physical danger. The retention of self-discipline . . . depends upon the maintaining of an appearance of discipline within the unit . . . When other men flee, the social pressure is lifted and the average soldier will respond as if he had been given a release from duty, for he knows that his personal failure is made inconspicuous by the general dissolution.[9]

And until the end of the Second World War, the armies were unaware that most of their soldiers, even if not running away, weren't actually killing anybody.

Basic Training

Tens of millions of men and growing numbers of women have seen combat, and yet there is something mysterious about it. The giving and receiving of death is not a normal transaction.

> The military makes demands which few if any other callings do, and of course emotionally disturbed people talk about being trained to kill . . . The whole essence of being a soldier is not to slay but to be slain. You offer yourself up to be slain, rather than setting yourself up as a slayer. Now one can get into very deep water here, but there's food for thought in it.
> General Sir John Hackett

To the layman, Hackett's definition of the "essence of being a soldier" sounds laughably romantic, but there really is food for thought in his words. Soldiers know they may die, but left to their own devices, most of them are remarkably reluctant to kill—and if they do kill, even in combat, many of them are deeply affected by it.

You think about it and you know you're going to have to kill but you don't understand the implications of that, because in the society in which you've lived murder is the most heinous of crimes ...

I was utterly terrified—petrified—but I knew there had to be a Japanese sniper in a small fishing shack near the shore ... and there was nobody else to go ... and so I ran towards the shack and broke in and found myself in an empty room.

There was a door which meant there was another room and the sniper was in that—and I just broke that down. I was just absolutely gripped by the fear that this man would expect me and would shoot me. But it turned out he was in a sniper harness and he couldn't turn around fast enough. He was entangled in the harness and so I shot him with a .45 and I felt remorse and shame. I can remember whispering foolishly, "I'm sorry" and then just throwing up ... I threw up all over myself. It was a betrayal of what I'd been taught since a child.

William Manchester

Manchester was a twenty-three-year-old corporal when he fought in Okinawa in 1945, and the idea of killing somebody had probably never crossed his mind until he fell into the hands of the US Marine Corps. Of course he was distressed by what he had done. The scoffers will say that his problem was just a "modern sensibility," pointing out that his seventeenth- and eighteenth-century ancestors regarded public executions as a form of entertainment. And if the shoe had been on the other foot, they will insist, the Japanese sniper would not have been equally upset by killing Manchester. Yet the armies themselves take the problem seriously.

"We are reluctant to admit that the business of war is killing," wrote S. L. A. Marshall in 1947, but today's armies are well aware that their recruits are at best reluctant killers. That's why they isolate their new recruits right away for a period of six to twelve weeks to do what they call "basic training." It has very little to do with teaching them how to use their weapons.

A new recruit responds to drill instructors, Marine Corps Recruitment Depot, San Diego

Basic training is a conversion process, in which the recruits are subjected to unremitting physical stress and psychological manipulation. The goal is to suppress their civilian identities and give them a whole new set of values, loyalties, and reflexes that will make them obedient and even willing soldiers. Generally it works, although the civilian identity is only submerged, not eradicated. Manchester killed as a trained soldier, but then reacted to his deed as the person he had been before.

"I guess you could say we brainwash them a little bit," said a US Marine drill instructor at Parris Island, the Marines' East Coast training base, a full two generations later, "but they're good kids." They have always been good kids, but until the end of the Second World War the military didn't realize that most of them stayed unwilling to kill after all their training. It was the same S. L. A. Marshall, then a colonel serving as a combat historian, who discovered through post-combat interviews with American infantry units in both the Pacific and European theaters in 1944–45 that only a quarter or less of the soldiers had fired their personal weapons even in intense combat. They did not run away but, said Marshall, when the moment came, they could not bring themselves to kill.

Natural-Born Killers?

> The man who can endure the mental and physical stresses of combat still has such an inner and usually unrealized resistance towards killing a fellow man that he will not of his own volition take life if it is possible to turn away from that responsibility . . . At the vital point, he becomes a conscientious objector.
>
> S. L. A. Marshall, *Men Against Fire* (1947)

This came as a great surprise to the military, whose leadership had always assumed that most if not all soldiers in combat would fire at the enemy, if only to protect their own lives. But they took this problem very seriously and changed the way they trained their troops. Gone were the long, grassy firing ranges with bull's-eye targets at the end; soldiers now fire at pop-up targets of human figures that disappear again if the soldier has not fired in a couple of seconds. They call it "laying down reflex pathways."

They also addressed the soldiers' reluctance to kill in more direct ways. By the 1960s Marine Corps recruits were shouting

"Kill" every time their left foot came down as they ran during morning physical training sessions. The training seemed to work. As early as the Korean War in the early 1950s, Marshall reported that half the men were firing in combat, and by the late 1960s in the Vietnam War almost all the soldiers were allegedly firing their weapons during some perimeter defense crises.

Marshall assumed that the problem had only arisen during the Second World War because most soldiers were no longer directly supervised by their NCOs and officers on the battlefield. For most of history, the combat environment was an extremely crowded one. In a Roman legion, on the gun deck of an eighteenth-century ship of the line, or in a Napoleonic infantry battalion, men fought practically shoulder to shoulder. The presence of so many others going through the same ordeal imposed a huge moral pressure on each individual to do his part—and the presence of their NCOs meant that any shirking of their duty would immediately be punished, sometimes by death.

Even in the trenches of the First World War, the soldier had other men close around him, and could often see his whole company during an attack. But by the Second World War the lethality of artillery and machine-gun fire had forced infantrymen to disperse so widely that each man was effectively alone and unobserved in his own foxhole. In these lonely circumstances, Marshall theorized, the soldiers were free to avoid killing without bringing shame or punishment on themselves—and most therefore did just that—whereas the people on the machine-guns and other crew-served weapons, observed by their comrades, continued to do their duty as expected.

A logical implication of Marshall's discovery is that the reluctance to kill another human being is universal. If German and Japanese soldiers had been significantly more willing to kill, either because they'd been raised in a particularly warlike culture or because they had been more effectively brainwashed, they would have enjoyed immense superiority in the volume of aimed fire they produced, and would have won every battle they fought against American troops.

From a human point of view, it is good news that most people of every nationality and culture have a strong objection to killing other people, and avoid it if they can. It is less encouraging to learn how easily they can be tricked into doing it anyway by some elementary psychological conditioning and training. But after Marshall died there was a major academic effort to discredit his findings: his research methods were sloppy, the critics said; his results were distorted by wishful thinking; he just made it up.

There was substance in the criticism of his research methods, but a side effect of the controversy was to make people look for evidence of the same behavior in other times and places, and they found it. They found that many soldiers had been silently refusing to kill more than a century ago.

Ninety percent of the 25,574 abandoned muskets picked up after the Battle of Gettysburg (1863) in the American Civil War were loaded, which makes no sense if the soldiers who dropped them, presumably because they were killed or wounded, had been firing as soon as they loaded their weapons. Indeed, almost half the muskets—twelve thousand—were loaded more than once, and six thousand of them had between three and ten rounds loaded in the barrel, although the weapon would explode if actually fired in that state. The only rational explanation is that many men on both sides of the conflict were unable to evade the highly visible process of loading, but only mimicked the act of firing. And many more, we may presume, did load and fire, but just aimed high.

Major "Gabby" Gabreski in the cockpit of his P-47 Thunderbolt after his 28th kill (July 1944). He became an "ace" again in the Korean War.

A small minority of men appear to be "natural-born killers" who don't need to be persuaded. This doesn't mean they are murderers, but they do not feel the usual reluctance to kill when the circumstances make it necessary and even praiseworthy. For example, the US Air Force found that during the Second World War less than one percent of its fighter pilots became "aces" (the term originated in World War I, signifying that a pilot had destroyed at least five enemy aircraft); and they found that those few men accounted for between 30 and 40 percent of enemy aircraft shot down. Meanwhile the majority of its pilots never shot anybody down at all. There is no evidence that the majority were worse pilots; more likely they just lacked the killer instinct.

"They looked like ants"

As the average distance between the trigger finger and the target increases, the inhibitions of those who aren't natural-born killers drop away. Even five hundred meters will do it. Hein Severloh was a twenty-year-old *Wehrmacht* private manning a machine-gun overlooking Omaha Beach in Normandy when American troops came ashore on D-Day, June 6, 1944. His bunker was one of the few not destroyed by Allied bombing and naval gunfire, and his machine gun accounted for at least half of the 4,184 Americans who were killed or wounded in front of that bunker on Private Severloh's first and last day of combat. He fired it for nine hours, pausing only to change gun-barrels as they overheated, mowing down American soldiers as they exited their landing craft in the shallow water five hundred meters away.

"At that distance they looked like ants," said Severloh, and he felt no reluctance about what he was doing. But then one young American who had escaped the slaughter came running up the beach during a lull in the fighting, and Severloh picked up his rifle. The round smashed into the GI's forehead, sending his helmet spinning, and he slumped dead in the sand. At that distance, Severloh could see the contorted expression on his face. "It was only then I realized I had been killing people all the time," he said. "I still dream of that soldier now [in 2004]. I feel sick when I think about it."

If five hundred meters of distance provides a degree of insulation from the reality of what the weapons are doing to human beings, ten times that distance straight up makes it completely invisible.

It seemed as though the whole of Hamburg was on fire from one end to the other and a huge column of smoke was towering well above us—and we were on 20,000 feet!

Set in the darkness was a turbulent dome of bright red fire, lighted and ignited like the glowing heart of a vast brazier. I saw no streets, no outlines of buildings, only brighter fires which flared like yellow torches against a background of bright red ash. Above the city was a misty red haze. I looked down, fascinated but aghast, satisfied yet horrified . . . Our actual bombing was like putting another shovelful of coal into the furnace.

RAF aircrew over Hamburg, July 28, 1943[10]

Seventy-five years later, the bomber pilot of World War II has morphed into the Strategic Air Command "combat crew" doing correspondence courses for MBAs as they wait for the ICBM launch order that mercifully never comes, or the drone operator killing his or her "targets" on video from thousands of miles away.

Do Drone Pilots Dream of Exploding Sheep?

What I really like is the variety of prospects available to me. I get to play lots of different types of sport. And I think the pay is pretty good. I pay hardly anything on rent and bills, so more of the money I earn is my own. Flying UASs is great fun and puts us at the center of all missions in Afghanistan.

Online British army recruitment ad for "GUNNER—UNMANNED AERIAL SYSTEMS"[11]

The first armed drone attack was in 2001, but much-improved technology has led to a great acceleration in armed attacks since about 2008. In Afghanistan there were up to forty strikes a day in 2019, and the NGO Airwars estimated the total lives lost to drone strikes in Syria, Iraq, Yemen, Libya, and Somalia as of December 2020 at 55,506 people.[12] The United States Air Force is now training more people to fly Unmanned Aerial Vehicles (UAVs) than fighter and bomber pilots combined, and the scale and geographical scope of these "counterterrorist" operations has reignited the old, uneasy debate about the moral status of those who kill people (many of whom are civilians) from the sky.

The appalling casualties (around 50 percent fatalities) suffered by British, Canadian, and American bomber crews flying against Germany in World War II largely protected them from criticism about the morality of their actions, but drone pilots are not risking their own lives. Even inside the armed forces themselves, questions are being asked about their moral status, framed mostly as questions about whether they deserve to be granted the same honor and status as people who experience combat in person.

Even if the drone operators wear flight suits to work (as they do in some air forces), the real "war-fighters" do not want mere "cyber-warriors" to debase the currency of heroism that gives them value in their own eyes and those of others. A Pentagon proposal in 2013 to create a "Distinguished Warfare Medal" specifically for drone pilots that would rank above some US decorations for valor in combat caused outrage in armed forces and veterans' organizations. The American Legion's national commander, James E. Koutz, said his organization "still believes there's a fundamental difference between those who fight remotely, or via computer, and those fighting against an enemy who is trying to kill them."[13] The secretary of defense canceled the new medal after two months.

Among civilians, the concern is different. It is that this godlike technology enabling individuals to kill invisibly and invulnerably from the sky is morally deadening and will lead to huge abuses, especially as the operations are conducted with great secrecy. They rightly mistrust military enthusiasts like Air Marshal Greg Bagwell, a former Royal Air Force deputy commander of operations, who advocated recruiting "eighteen- and nineteen-year-olds straight out of the PlayStation bedroom" to operate the weapons.[14] But in fact the drone pilots of today are not morally dead. They are far more aware of exactly who their victims are and precisely what happens to them than were the young men high above Hamburg in 1943.

Most drone strikes today occur in the context of "counter-terrorist" and other counterinsurgency operations, in the midst of civilian societies that are not mobilized for war. Basic morality and the formal doctrines of counterinsurgency war both require that drone attacks against small groups of insurgents—and often single "terrorists"—do not cause mass casualties to the innocent people around them (including the families, friends, and neighbors of the targeted individuals). Drone operators typically spend hours or even days observing the daily lives of their targets so that they can first confirm their identities with confidence, and then find a time and place where they can be hit without endangering the lives of others.

That is the theory. The practice is sometimes less diligent, there is occasionally great time pressure, and many mistakes occur that take innocent lives. But drone operators often do get to "know" their targets, and even their families, before the kill is made. They may also be required to loiter in the area afterward to see if the target was killed, who comes to the funeral, etc.— to say nothing of the oft-denied "double-tap" attacks that take out the rescuers and/or mourners later the same day. The lives of the operators are never at risk, and investigations by the USAF School of Aerospace Medicine have shown that they are no more prone to PTSD (post-traumatic stress disorder) than other service members who have not been exposed to combat: around 2 to 5 percent, which is not far off the twelve-month prevalence of PTSD in US civilian adults. Many drone operators do, however, suffer from powerful emotional reactions to what they have seen and done, and 11 percent reported high levels of "psychological distress."[15]

The term "moral injury" is gradually gaining ground in military medical circles (against considerable resistance) to describe this distress. In an unpublished paper, one former drone operator linked this phenomenon to "cognitive combat intimacy," a relational attachment forged through close observation of violent events in high resolution. In one passage, he described a scenario in which an operator executed a strike that killed a "terrorist facilitator" while sparing his child. Afterward "the child walked back to the pieces of his father and began to place the pieces back into human shape," to the horror of the operator. The more they watched their targets go about their daily lives—getting dressed, playing with their kids—the greater their "risk of moral injury," he concluded.[16]

In all these operations human beings are still in the loop. It's what comes next that really worries people.

The LAWS of War

I suspect we could have an army of 120,000 [in the 2030s], of which 30,000 might be robots, who knows?
General Sir Nick Carter, British Chief of Defense Staff, November 2020[17]

The British armed forces are having trouble recruiting enough people to meet even their current authorized manpower limit of 82,050, so one can understand their interest in nonhuman supplements. Most militaries in developed countries face a similar problem. Moreover, "robots" can be programmed to perform tasks in battle that would cost too many lives if humans had to do them, and if they are "killed" in large numbers they do not provoke the kind of political backlash at home that accompanies high human casualties. But if the behavior of these robots in combat has to be supervised by human beings, there is no saving of manpower, and a great loss in reaction time. In particular, kill/don't kill decisions need to be taken in a split second.

The unwelcome but unavoidable conclusion is that, in order to be useful in combat, these robots must be what is known as "lethal autonomous weapons systems" (LAWS), free to make their own killing decisions. This would take us deep into "Terminator" country, where nobody in their right mind would want to go. Or rather, they would never go there if you put the choice like that, but of course that's not how it would ever be stated in practice (and the weapons in question would not resemble Arnold Schwarzenegger in the slightest).

None of these hypothetical LAWS will become a reality before considerable advances have been made in artificial intelligence (facial recognition software may be coming along nicely, but few robots can even dance yet). It will be very hard to design weaponized robots to operate safely (from their own side's point of view) in the complex battle spaces created by human armies, but very big and largely ungoverned spaces that shelter extremists or rebels will present tempting opportunities for earlier deployment. Ten thousand next-but-one-generation LAWS with no requirement for drone pilots could track and winnow insurgents in the rural parts of a country the size of Afghanistan at a quite reasonable cost.

At $5 million a copy for mass-produced, state-of-the-art LAWS drones, a capital outlay of $50 billion spread over five years with a recurrent annual spend of $10 billion will buy you a killer drone to cover each five-by-five-mile area of rural Afghanistan—all for a fraction of the US "war funding" budget.* Any sign of insurgent activity, such as carrying a weapon, and the target gets zapped. There will be collateral damage, of course, but you're not talking about your fellow countrymen here, so how much do you really care, given the miserable available policy alternatives?

We are probably a decade or more away from a mature LAWS technology, but unless there is an international consensus to ban it in the relatively near future it will come to pass. It will not necessarily be the United States that crosses the Rubicon: once any major power acquires the technology, the others will surely follow.

The impact on large-scale, high-intensity warfare may prove quite modest, since in that kind of war even human decision-makers are free to kill with little restraint, but the effect on counterinsurgency operations could be very great. LAWS would lessen political pressure to end "forever wars" in places like Afghanistan or Somalia, and ruthless autocratic regimes would have a powerful new tool to help them hang on to power indefinitely.

Poison gas and biological weapons have been outlawed with some success by international treaty, and less formal international understandings have largely eliminated pernicious but not decisive weapons like land mines and blinding laser technology. Lethal autonomous weapons systems are not yet

---

* This is currently c. $69 billion per year and is supplementary to the defense budget.

David Wreckham on an anti-killer robot leafletting drive outside the British parliament in April 2019

inevitable, and a network of NGOs led by the Campaign to Stop Killer Robots has been working since 2013 to put a United Nations–backed ban on LAWS on the international agenda. At the time of writing, thirty countries have explicitly supported such a ban, and another sixty-seven have expressed a positive interest in it.[18]

But we are getting ahead of ourselves.

CHAPTER 3

The Evolution of Battle

3500–1500 BCE

The First Army Battles

We don't know when the first battle between real armies took place, but it was probably around 5,500 years ago in the land of Sumer, in today's Iraq. The armies of that time would have carried the same weapons that hunters and warriors had been using on animals and each other for millennia—spears, knives, axes, perhaps bows and arrows— but they would be ten or twenty times more numerous than any hunter-gatherer band, and they would actually stand and fight, obeying a single commander, at least for a few minutes. Hunter-gatherers could never have done such a thing; only farmers had the numbers, the commitment, and the right social structure.

It is possible, however, that there was one very early exception. In the 1950s archaeologists discovered that Jericho had become the first walled town in the world over ten thousand years ago, between 8500 and 8000 BCE. The town walls were at least twelve feet high and six feet thick, with a rock-cut moat ten feet deep at their base, and they encircled an area of ten acres. Up to three thousand people lived behind the walls, and there was a twenty-five-foot-high tower in the middle that probably served as a final refuge or keep for the most important residents. The walls are rather elaborate for mere flood defenses and suggest that this may have been a militarized society, defending something that other people wanted badly enough to attack it. This great asset was the Jericho aquifer, which spilled its water out over a series of natural terraces around the city.

Jericho's walls appeared at the end of a two-thousand-year period when local "Natufian" hunter-gatherers in the Fertile Crescent, while continuing to hunt wild game, were devoting more and more of their time to harvesting wild plants. Their semi-permanent settlements included grain-storage pits, but around 8500 BCE a shift to drier climatic conditions dramatically shrank the number of settlements. The consequent food shortages may have driven the Natufians to shift from merely reaping wild grains to deliberately sowing them; and they may also have led to one or more attempts by hungry tribes to seize control of the Jericho aquifer, for whoever controlled the aquifer would still have water and therefore food. All of which could explain those ten-thousand-year-old walls, but the crisis passed and there is no evidence of other city walls in the Fertile Crescent for another three thousand years. Real battles were a long time in the making.

The next town we know of, almost a thousand years later and six hundred miles north of Jericho, is Çatal Hüyük, a community of five to seven thousand people that thrived near what is now Konya in southern Turkey between 7100 BCE and 5700 BCE. The houses were built in a honeycomb-like structure, with no streets or alleys between and entrances high on the walls or in the roofs. There were no defenses that could have withstood a serious army even for a day.

There were storage bins for wheat and barley, so some kind of agriculture was underway, but the inhabitants also depended on hunting game and gathering wild plants, fruits, and nuts in the river valley. They had certainly domesticated goats, and there are hints that they were also working on cattle. The absence of larger dwellings or ceremonial buildings suggest that they were still an egalitarian society, and grave goods indicate that women had similar status to men. All in all, they look very like the descendants of some hunter-gatherer bands who decided to get together and move indoors.

This was the era, between 6000 BCE and 4000 BCE, when all the "founder crops" and goats, sheep, pigs, and cattle were being domesticated, but few people were following the example of Çatal Hüyük and creating "proto-urban settlements." The exception was Sumer, the wetlands along the lower Euphrates River in what was later known to the Greeks as Mesopotamia and is now called Iraq. Mesopotamia is a flat, almost featureless plain created by the Tigris and Euphrates, the two rivers that drain most of the upland part of the Fertile Crescent. The soil was amazingly fertile: it was pure silt laid down by past flooding. You could easily get two crops a year off this land, but the people who settled in Sumer were not yet full-time farmers.

The last stretch of the lower Euphrates was a hunter-gatherer's paradise: the Garden of Eden, if you like. At that time it was immensely rich and varied in its food sources, allowing what were dense populations by hunter-gatherer standards to live together while still pursuing a traditional lifestyle, catching fish and mollusks, hunting migratory birds and deer, gathering wild plants, and doing a little low-impact agriculture on the side—just spread your seed where you know the river will flood, and wait for it to grow in the rich silt that's left behind when it recedes.

The earliest settlers of Sumer all spoke essentially the same language, but they created at least a dozen settlements that had grown into little city-states by the early fourth millennium BCE. Wars, however, were not frequent or severe, for the Sumerians very early hit upon the device of using religion as a nonmilitary source of authority to settle disputes. They didn't have kings or permanent secular leaders, but they did have temple priests whose role, apart from pleasing the gods, was to settle disputes peacefully not only among the local residents but also between neighboring settlements. Their occasional wars were fought in the classic hunter-gatherer style, and their city walls (if they had them: there is no evidence of their existence) would have been to discourage raids. Really massive ramparts did not start going up until much later.

The temple priests bought Sumer five, maybe ten centuries of relative peace—but the growing populations ultimately made inter-city conflicts inevitable. The population was rising fast because women in these new settlements no longer had to restrict their childbearing to one surviving baby every four years (nomadic mothers can't carry around two small children). When the climate hit another dry phase around 3500 BCE and wild food sources dwindled, people had to turn to farming—but good farmland was becoming scarce because the rivers were not flooding as high or as long. The cities—only a two

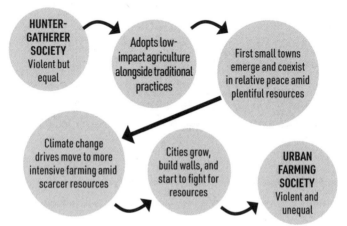

or three days' walk apart—started to fight over it, and by 3200 BCE walls were going up around the world's biggest city, Uruk (population 25,000–50,000). Soon other major Sumerian cities like Kish, Nippur, Lagash, Eridu, and Ur also had walls.[1]

This new urban lifestyle offered lots of opportunities for clever or lucky people to accumulate property of various sorts, including land, and a gap began to open between the rich and the rest. Some people were now much more equal than others, and the rest simply had to lump it.

For one group, though, there was an alternative.

A New Way of Life

It was almost certainly settled communities that first domesticated sheep, goats, and cattle, but these tamed animals created the possibility of a new and different way of life: pastoralism. People could regain their independence by herding tamed animals and using their meat, hide, wool, milk, and blood to support an entirely independent lifestyle. Some would have been greatly tempted by this option, because the values and traditions of free men and women were being eroded fast in the agricultural societies.

Most people had to accept the new rules, but the people who looked after the animals had a choice. They lived on the fringes of the farming community anyway, to keep the animals from eating or trampling the crops, and they regularly disappeared off into the uplands in spring to find fresh pasture. At some point, it must have occurred to the herders that they didn't have to come back.

Pastoralism is a harsh way of life, without a roof over your head or much in the way of material possessions, but it would have attracted those who didn't like what was happening in the settled communities. During the fourth and third millennia BCE, pastoral societies were coming into existence throughout the Middle East. The "nomads" as they were called, would always be greatly outnumbered by the farmers, and they would always depend on the settled societies for their higher technologies, including their metal weapons. But it was a viable alternative to the cramped farming lifestyle, and from the start the nomads had a deep contempt for the settled folk.

It's likely that these pastoralists soon started raiding each others' herds, but a more attractive option would have been to steal the farmers' animals—and while they were at it, all the other valuable things that farmers had and they didn't. It was tempting, and it was easy.

The nomads didn't have horses yet, but even on foot they were far more mobile than farmers. Since their animals moved with them, they could concentrate all their fighting strength against a chosen target at short notice. Farmers couldn't do that, so it was the nomads who generally had numbers on their side at the chosen place on the right day. Their modus operandi would have been a surprise raid followed by a rapid retreat into the highlands with the spoils—and since they couldn't retreat very fast on foot with all their animals, they would have taken steps to discourage pursuit. The obvious steps were terror, atrocity, and massacre.

Ruthless Nomads?

Fighting between groups who recognize their common humanity is generally constrained by custom and ritual, while the same groups approach hunting wild animals in a more ruthlessly pragmatic spirit: deceive the animal, then kill it. The psychological relationship between nomads and farmers was similar: the settled peoples were seen as lesser beings, no longer fully human. As prey to the nomad predators, they could be killed without compunction, and the whole history of attacks by nomads on farming peoples is one of remorseless cruelty and contempt by the former toward the latter.

This could be another explanation for the walls. It wouldn't take many terrifying attacks to cause a wave of wall-building among the farming communities—and a wave of militarization too. Indeed, some historians have argued that such raids were the main driver behind the growing intensity of warfare between settled communities, as the farmers gradually imported nomad ruthlessness into their own conflicts.[2]

If you are fighting nomads, the penalty for losing is close to total. So we can imagine a gradual rise in the discipline demanded of the individual warrior and the control exercised by the commander, because these changes bring more success in battle. Against nomadic raiders, these new, more efficient ways of fighting were indispensable—but once people had worked them out, would they revert to the old, inefficient ways in the increasingly frequent wars with rival farming communities? Of course not. And thus the lethality of battle started to rise.

Organized Slaughter

Meriones pursued and overtaking [Pheraklos]
struck in the right buttock and the spearhead drove straight
on and passing under the bone went into the bladder.
He dropped, screaming, to his knees, and death was a mist
about him.
Meges . . . killed Pedaios . . .
Struck him the sharp spear behind the head at the tendon
and straight on through the teeth and under the tongue cut the
bronze blade
and he dropped in the dust gripping in his teeth the cold bronze.

> *Euryplos ... killed brilliant Hypsenor ...*
> *Running in chase as he fled before him struck in the shoulder*
> *with a blow swept from the sword and cut the arm's weight*
> *from him,*
> *so that the arm dropped bleeding to the ground, and the red death*
> *and destiny the powerful took hold of both eyes.*
> *So they went at their work all about the mighty encounter.*
>
> Homer, *Iliad*[3]

The battle under the walls of Troy, as described above, actually took place circa 1200 BCE, but he composed his epic poem around 800 BCE. Homer obeys the conventions of his culture and describes the battle in terms of single combat between named heroes, but that is not what actually happens on the ground. This is the war of infantry phalanxes—the first real armies—and it is indeed a mighty encounter.

The men in an infantry phalanx are doing something that has never before been asked of people. Holding spears and shields, they have to form three or more straight lines hundreds or even thousands of men long. They have to stay in that formation, despite any bumps or hollows in the ground, until they make contact with the enemy, who is arrayed in an equally unwieldy manner—and once the two phalanxes collide they must push and stab, with the leading edge of the two formations eroding moment by moment as men go down, until one side panics and tries to retreat. But there are other lines of men behind who have not yet caught the panic and continue to press forward, so the cohesion of the losing formation crumbles. Once that happens it is doomed: the men attempting to flee find themselves trapped in their own crowd and are cut down from behind.

It is this last and ugliest phase of the battle that Homer is describing, with "heroes" being cut down from behind as they

THE SHORTEST HISTORY OF WAR

try to escape. The elevated "warrior" verse sets the epic tone, but the reality is one of frightened young men running for their lives and not making it. It is ruthless, deliberate slaughter on an unprecedented scale, and it began not in the age when Homer lived or even when he set his great poem, but over a millenium earlier in the rival city-states of Mesopotamia.

Detail from the Stele of the Vultures, c. 2500 BCE

You can see a phalanx on the Stele of the Vultures, the first representation of a Mesopotamian army, dating from around 2500 BCE. Eannatum, the ruler of Lagash, is leading his army out to battle, and behind him are the soldiers of the city. They are shoulder to shoulder, their shields overlapping, several rows deep, with the spears of all the rows bristling ahead of the formation. Almost certainly, they are marching in step. When they met the enemy formation, from the neighboring city of Umma, there would have been a brief but savage face-to-face struggle, certainly less than five minutes, followed by the slaughter of the phalanx that broke first. The Stele of the Vultures claims that three thousand men of the army of Umma died on the battlefield—and those who were captured were marched to the foot of their own city's walls and slaughtered.

More People, More Cities, More Wars

The willingness of large numbers of men to stand their ground despite the high probability that they will die there in the next five minutes has no precedent in the long human, primate, or even mammalian past. To find anything comparable, we must go to the battles fought between ant colonies, but at least the ants have the excuse of a shared genetic heritage. Nomad attacks may have been responsible for a general trend toward greater ruthlessness in war, but that does not get us all the way to the astounding discipline and bravery of a city-state's phalanx.

The saga of Gilgamesh, ruler of the city-state of Uruk about 2700 BCE, may be showing us some of this process. Written history is kicking in, so at last we have some names, dates, and stories, and center-stage at once is the hero Gilgamesh, who becomes the big man (*"lugal"*) or king of Uruk. The epic is the usual quest story—Gilgamesh seeks eternal life—combined with some encrypted renderings of local politics in twenty-seventh-century BCE Uruk. Reading between the lines, it seems likely that he subverted the old, participatory institutions of Uruk—a senate-like assembly of elders and a general body of all adult men—and turned them to his own purposes. Exploiting a quarrel with Kish and using a combination of rhetoric and threats, Gilgamesh persuaded these assemblies to accept his ascendancy over the city. But even after gaining power, Gilgamesh did not become an absolute monarch: he had to keep the people on his side, and most of them probably continued to see themselves not as mere subjects of his will, but as full citizens. He couldn't just order them around.

The epic may be a snapshot of a transitional stage. Property and social class were now setting some people above others, but the myth of equality lived on in the assembly of all adult males. Allowing for two thousand years of technological and cultural differences, the city-states of early Sumer *were* the Greek city-states of early classical times: the rich and well-born generally got their way in the end, but the proprieties of public consultation and consensus in assemblies of all citizens capable of bearing arms still had to be observed.[4] This precarious survival of egalitarian values may be what made phalanxes possible, for if the whole adult male population felt involved in the decision to go to war, then you could legitimately demand that they follow through by putting their lives on the line.

The phalanx was an awesomely effective military tool, and it was also cheap. The soldiers in the ranks could be trained to use their simple shields and spears effectively and to move in tight formations in one free afternoon a week. Bronze spearheads were the only significant expense in equipping them, although the better-off members of the community would certainly invest in bronze helmets and shin protection as well. It's one of history's great bargains: a truly effective military force, practically unstoppable except by another phalanx, for little more than a song.

As the centuries passed and the tyrannies deepened in the Sumerian cities, the phalanx style of warfare eroded and vanished, because absolute monarchs preferred to fight battles with standing armies of hired soldiers, leaving the mass of the citizenry unarmed, untrained, and politically inert. By the latter part of the third millennium, phalanxes had virtually disappeared from Mesopotamian battlefields. But the battles continued.

The thirteen city-states of classic Sumer existed for many centuries in a permanent state of alternating hot and cold wars with their neighbors. They had fallen unwittingly into a balance-of-power system in which most players survived, but at a high cost. If you were on the losing side, you would just hang on until some of the other players got nervous about the growing strength of the big winners and changed sides to contain their power. Yanomamo villagers would recognize what was happening; it was just on a far larger scale.

The balance-of-power system produces frequent wars, but it has lasted, with only rare interruptions, for five thousand years. It was the organizing principle in the global rivalries of the early twentieth-century great powers as much as it was in the local squabbles of the Sumerian city-states. The alliances would shift but the wars were a constant: since 1800, Britain and France, France and Germany, the United States and Britain have all been both enemies and allies. Kish, Shuruppak, Ur, Nippur, and Lagash were doubtless just as fickle in their loyalties, although we don't know the details of their local game. And although people told themselves each time that the war was about something specific—"The War of the Spanish Succession" or "The War of Jenkins' Ear"—it was really the system itself that produced the wars.

Modern nation-states went to war, on average, about once per generation in the period 1800–1945, and were at war for about one year in five during the entire period. National sovereignty makes every state exclusively responsible for its own survival, which it can only ensure by having enough military power, generally obtained by making alliances with other states. Sooner or later you are bound to get it wrong—your allies betray you, your forces are in the wrong place—which is why at least 90 percent of the states that ever existed have been destroyed by war.

So what became of the conflict depicted and described on the Stele of the Vultures—Lagash versus Umma, whose phalanxes clashed some time around 2500 BCE, leaving three thousand men from Umma dead on the battlefield? The two city-states were trying to establish their hegemony over all of Sumer, and the strategic advantage swung back and forth for 150 years as battles were lost or won and their allies repeatedly changed sides. In the end the army of Umma triumphed, sacked the city of Lagash, looted its temple, and lorded it over Sumer for a few years. Then Umma itself was conquered by a new phenomenon: the world's first military empire.

The First Military Empire

> Sargon, the Mighty King, King of Akkad, am I.
> He who keeps Travelling the Four Lands

By the mid-2300s BCE, newcomers speaking Semitic languages were moving down from the Eastern Mediterranean area occupied today by Syria, Lebanon, Jordan, and Israel into the fertile Mesopotamian plains and setting up their own cities, but Sargon, though of Semitic origin, grew up in the old Sumerian city of Kish. He rose to become cup-bearer to King Ur-Zababa before seizing power himself in a coup whose details remain unknown. He conquered Uruk, then all the other cities of Sumer, then the upland kingdoms of Elam, Mari, and Ebla. He appointed governors, installed permanent garrisons, drew up tax lists in each new conquered province, and created a centrally controlled bureaucracy to run it from his newly built capital, Akkad. It was the world's first multinational empire.

Sargon's army was a professional, multiethnic force of considerable size: one of his inscriptions boasts that 5,400 men daily took their meals in his presence. It was the first army that could campaign far from home, since it had a logistical train to bring supplies up behind it. It could capture heavily fortified cities by undermining the walls or going over the top on scaling ladders.

Scythians shooting with composite bows, Kerch, Crimea, 4th century BCE

Sargon's soldiers probably never fought in a classic phalanx formation. It would have been a waste of their special talents. These men had the time and the skill to master not only the spear but also the composite bow, a recent innovation that would remain the best projectile weapon for thousands of years to come. They could even fight from war chariots. His army won almost every time.

Sargon of Akkad was the prototype of Alexander, Napoleon, and Hitler: a man who set out to conquer the world, or at least the parts of it that seemed important at the time. His propagandists boasted that his empire ran "from the Lower Sea to the Upper Sea" (from the Gulf to the Mediterranean), but nothing held it together except military power. The conquered cities and provinces rebelled whenever his army was committed elsewhere, and Sargon's successors were eventually worn down by the ceaseless effort to preserve his empire. The city of Akkad itself was destroyed in 2159 BCE. Other empires, however, followed in unending succession.

Anthill Society

By 2000 BCE the overwhelming majority of human beings were farmers, and almost all lived in states that were extravagantly unequal, with semidivine kings at the top and a mass of serfs and slaves at the bottom. Was this the inevitable consequence of living in mass societies?

The answer, probably, is yes. The problem of numbers was insoluble and would remain so for a very long time.

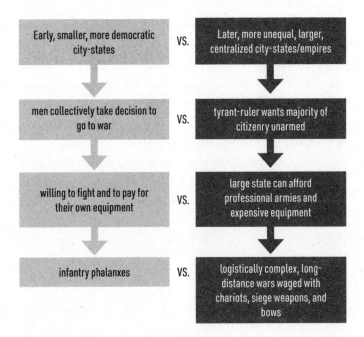

Egalitarianism works in small societies where everybody knows everybody else; where would-be alpha males can be spotted and neutralized before they get too powerful; and where decisions can be debated face-to-face until a consensus emerges. None of this works if your new style of life requires you to live in far bigger groups. New tools like writing, money, and bureaucracy could help to manage these large new societies, but there was no way traditional human politics could continue. What works for a society of forty people cannot work for a society of forty thousand, let alone four million. Until and unless some innovation comes along that enables huge numbers of people to make decisions together, the old political system is dead. So is equality.

The only system that did work was one in which orders were passed down from the top and slavishly obeyed at the bottom. The social structure of the average ancient empire was closer to the anthill than to our own hunter-gatherer past. Yet the empires were always unstable, because human beings had not actually become ants; behind the bitten tongues and the bowed heads they remained the same people they had always been. Physical force, or at least the permanent threat of force, was needed to keep all these newly tamed heirs of the hunter-gatherers in line, so militarization and tyranny became almost universal.

Most of the people of the agricultural mass societies were stunted and bent by poor diet and endless labor. Women were the biggest losers, reduced to social inferiority and confined to narrow lives of endless childbearing, but few men would freely choose the life of a peasant farmer over that of a traditional hunter either. Thousands of years later, the experiment of civilization would eventually pay off for at least some of its children, but from the standpoint of 2000 BCE it was a human disaster. Then things got worse.

Steppe Change: Horses and Wheels

There has been more than one Dark Age. The first was between about 2000 and 1500 BCE, when pastoral peoples equipped with war chariots conquered all the centers of civilization in Eurasia. For most of recorded history the civilized societies of the Old World were relatively small areas with dense farming populations—in China, northern India, the Middle East, and Europe—that lay just south or west of the steppes, the five thousand-mile-wide "sea of grass" stretching from southern Russia to Manchuria. This was the home of the horse nomads, who periodically burst out of their heartland to smash those civilizations.

Two things enabled these people to colonize the million-and-a-half square miles of the grasslands. The first was horses, domesticated in the southern Ukraine some time before 4000 BCE. They were far smaller and weaker in the back than modern horses, but they enabled the pastoral peoples to move their herds deeper into the grasslands. The second was the wheel, invented around 3300 BCE, which let them load their belongings into wagons.

Possible chariot on the Bronocile pot, Poland, c. 3500 BCE

The nomadic steppe culture that would spawn endless conquerors over the next three thousand years may have sprung into being in only a couple of centuries. But once the pastoral peoples had filled the grasslands to their carrying capacity (perhaps only three to five million people), they came back to conquer the civilized lands.

Their favorite weapons system combined the chariot, invented in the civilized lands as early as 2300 BCE, with the new composite bow, which was longer-range, faster-shooting, and above all smaller (and therefore perfect for use from a chariot).[5] Previously, their raids had relied on surprise and a temporary local superiority in numbers, but now they could actually fight civilized armies and win, especially as the highly motivated volunteer phalanxes of the early city-states had gone the way of the egalitarian values they'd relied upon. The nomads' advantage was not just their weapons; it was also the fact that they were herdsmen, accustomed to controlling flocks of animals.

It was flock management, as much as slaughter and butchery, which made the pastoralists so cold-bloodedly adept at confronting the sedentary agriculturalists of the civilized lands in battle . . . [Civilized] battle formations were likely to have been loose, discipline weak and battlefield behavior crowd- or herd-like. Working a herd, however, was the pastoralists' stock in trade. They knew how to break a flock up into manageable sections, how to cut off a line of retreat by circling to a flank, how to compress scattered beasts into a compact mass, how to isolate flock-leaders, how to dominate superior numbers by threat and menace, how to kill the chosen few while leaving the mass inert and subject to control.

John Keegan, *A History of Warfare*[6]

First the nomads would harass the defenders with showers of arrows, only committing themselves to a decisive attack when the enemy began to flee.

> Circling at a distance of 100 or 200 yards from the herds of unarmored foot soldiers, a chariot crew—one to drive, one to shoot—might have transfixed six men a minute. Ten minutes' work by ten chariots would cause 500 casualties or more, a Battle of the Somme-like toll among the small armies of the period.
>
> John Keegan, ibid.[7]

They were almost impossible for the armies of the early empires to deal with. Hammurabi's Amorite empire, which ruled most of Mesopotamia from his capital of Babylon, was overwhelmed by the Kassite and Hurrian charioteers flooding in from the highland area that is now Kurdistan in the sixteenth century BCE. The Hurrians spoke an Indo-European language, as did the Hittite charioteers who conquered most of central Anatolia (today's Turkey) to the west around 1600 BCE. Still farther to the west, the Mycenaeans who swept down the Balkans into Greece had the same chariots and spoke another Indo-European language.

The relatively nonmilitarized Egyptian kingdom was conquered for the first time ever in the eighteenth century BCE by the Hyksos, chariot-driving pastoralists from northwestern Arabia who spoke a Semitic language. Far to the east the Aryans, an Indo-European people originating on the Iranian plateau, replaced the early civilization of the Indus valley and established their rule over most of northern India. The origins of the Shang dynasty in northern China around 1700 BCE are disputed, but the sudden appearance of chariots in a part of the world where there had previously been no wheeled transport of any kind suggests that the founders of the Shang state may have been other Indo-European pastoralists.[8]

The nomad conquerors were tiny minorities ruling over hostile populations with the help of enslaved administrators. (They themselves had neither writing nor bureaucracy.) In some places they stayed in power less than a century: the Egyptians drove the Hyksos out in 1567 BCE, and the Hurrian overlords of Babylon were overthrown by the Assyrian king Ashur-uballit in 1365 BCE. The founders of the Shang dynasty were quickly absorbed by the vastly more sophisticated Chinese culture, and presented themselves to the world as a native Chinese dynasty.

Even where the language and culture of the invaders eventually prevailed (as in Greece, in Hittite Anatolia, and in Aryan-ruled India), within a few generations they were not really pastoralists anymore, though the modern Indian caste system is an echo of the system of slavery and serfdom with which they secured their hold on power. And whether the invaders stayed in power or not, their impact was enormous; after this first Dark Age, almost everybody was militarized.

CHAPTER 4

Classical War

1500 BCE–1400 CE

Constant Changeless War

While the dawn civilizations were building a brave new world of farms and cities and armies, major innovations in warfare were happening at the headlong rate of one every couple of centuries: large fortifications, phalanxes, composite bows, siege machinery, chariots, cavalry, etc. Once all these major elements of "classical" warfare were in place, however, the pace of change slowed right down.

War was constant, and almost changeless. At the end of the Bronze Age in 1200–1150 BCE there was another, briefer Dark Age marked by the collapse of most Middle Eastern civilizations, but the subsequent transition to iron weapons did not bring any significant changes in military tactics. Indeed, many historians would agree that a well-trained army with competent commanders from 500 BCE would stand a fighting chance against a comparable army from 1400 CE. Let the earlier armies swap their bronze weapons for iron ones and you could probably push this comparison back as far as 1500 BCE.

The Assyrians, based in northern Mesopotamia, had that kind of army. It was almost modern in its structure, with military engineers, supply depots, transport columns, and bridging equipment. It could move fast on the royal highways that were maintained throughout the empire, and campaign as far as three hundred miles away from its base. It was the first army to incorporate effective siege machinery, to equip its soldiers with iron armor and weapons, and to supplement its chariots with a force of horse-riding cavalry. And it was campaigning almost all the time.

Assyria waxed and waned over the centuries, as any empire with no natural geographical, historical, or ethnic borders is likely to do. Under Shalmaneser I and his son Tukulti-Ninurta I (1274–1208 BCE), the empire spread in every direction and reached the Persian Gulf in the south, only to collapse back to the core area after their deaths. In the final three hundred years of its history it became a purely military enterprise, permanently at war and terrorizing the whole Middle East to ensure a constant flow of booty and tribute to its treasury.

The Assyrians deported whole populations amid appalling massacres and resettled them far from home in punishment for rebellions: the Israelites were not the only people to suffer this fate. Assyria's army grew to the astonishing total (for the times) of 120,000 men, able to wage several campaigns at once, and its kings and commanders cultivated a reputation for extreme cruelty. We know of the Assyrians' addiction to sadism mainly from their own inscriptions; they boasted about it.

> The commander-in-chief of the king of Elam, together with his nobles . . . I cut their throats like sheep . . . My prancing steeds, trained to harness, plunged into their welling blood as into a river; the wheels of my battle chariots were bespattered with blood and filth . . . [In their terror] they passed scalding urine and voided their excrement in their chariots.
>
> Sennacherib, King of Assyria, 691 BCE[1]

In the end, the Assyrian empire was consumed by war. When the Medes, new nomad invaders, rode into the Middle East in the seventh century BCE—genuine cavalry this time, not charioteers, for selective breeding had finally produced horses strong enough to carry a rider in the forward "control" position—Assyria's civilized enemies joined forces with the nomads to bring the hated empire down: in 612 BCE the Assyrian capital, Nineveh, was destroyed so totally that its location has been lost to posterity.[2]

Siege Warfare

An ancient city was falling and the long years of her empire were at an end. Everywhere the dead lay motionless about the streets . . . Greeks were dashing to the (palace), and thronging round the entrance with their shields locked together over their backs: ladders were already firmly in place against the walls, and the attackers even now putting their weight on the rungs near the door-lintels. Holding shields on their left arms thrust forward for protection, with their right hands they grasped the roof. To oppose them the Trojans, on the brink of death and knowing their plight was desperate, sought to defend themselves by tearing up tiles from the roof-tops of houses . . . to use as missiles . . . Inside the palace there was sobbing and a confused and pitiful uproar. The building rang from end to end with the anguished cries of women.

Publius Vergilius Maro (Virgil), c. 19 BCE[3]

This is Troy, whose fall is traditionally dated to 1183 BCE, a time when history was rapidly transformed into legend. The story of the Trojan Horse may even be a garbled account of the siege machinery that finally breached the city's walls, for the Achaean Greeks besieging Troy could easily have hired military engineers from one of the more civilized countries to the east: at this time the fall of the Hittite empire would have left a lot of unemployed professional soldiers around Asia Minor. If Hittite mercenaries had built a siege tower for the attackers—a wooden structure several stories high, mounted on wheels, with a hide-covered roof and a metal-tipped battering ram slung in the interior—the Achaeans might well have dubbed it a wooden horse, leaving subsequent generations to embellish the story. (A siege tower pictured in a roughly contemporary Assyrian bas-relief does look somewhat like a giant horse.)

Siege tower on Assyrian bas-relief, NW Palace of Nimrud, c. 865–860 BCE

Troy was actually destroyed after a long siege, but Homer did not compose his epic poem about it until four centuries later. Virgil wrote his vivid account of the sack of Troy eight centuries after that, in a personalized style that would never have been used by those who lived through the event. The details of his narrative are fiction, but he knew what must have happened because he lived in a world where some unfortunate city had met its end like this every few years for as long as memory ran.

Carthage, for example, was stormed by Roman troops in 146 BCE after a three-year siege at the end of the Third Punic

War. There is an eyewitness account of how the despairing, half-starved Carthaginians held out inside the city through six days of street fighting.

> Three streets leading from the market place to the citadel were lined on both sides with six-storey houses, from which the Romans were pelted. They seized the first houses and from their roofs they made bridges of planks and beams to cross over to the next. While one battle was in progress on the roofs, another was fought, against all comers, in the street below. Everywhere there was groaning and wailing and shouting and agony of every description. Some were killed out of hand, some flung down alive from the roofs to the pavement, and of those some were caught on upright spears . . .
>
> Appian (based on Polybius's eyewitness account)[4]

The relatively few Carthaginians who survived the sack of their city (population c. 300,000) were sold into slavery, and the devastated site was formally cursed and sprinkled with salt by the victorious Roman general. It remained uninhabited until a Roman colony was founded on the ruins over a century later. All this leaves an impression of berserk violence and insane vindictiveness, which is precisely the impression that the victorious Romans wanted to leave.

The Phalanx Returns

> In the battle line each man requires a lateral space of three feet, while the distance between ranks is six feet. Thus, 10,000 men can be placed in a rectangle about 1,500 yards by twelve yards.
>
> Vegetius on Roman tactics[5]

Battles determined the course of our ancestors' lives, and they were no less clever than we are. If for several thousand years they could think of no better way to fight than massed in shoulder-to-shoulder formations, there had to be a good reason. There have been enough desperate men with nothing left to lose on the countless battlefields of the past that almost everything got tried sooner or later. And nothing, until well after the introduction of firearms, worked better than the organization and tactics that were already more or less standard before the time of Alexander the Great.

Vegetius is describing a Roman version of a phalanx because by the middle of the first millennium BCE, the formation had once again become widespread. It had gone out of fashion with the rise of the "oriental empires," but as the centers of wealth and power moved west from the Fertile Crescent to the rising city-states of Greece and Rome, large numbers of men with civic patriotism and high motivation were becoming available—and against the troops of another civilized state who would stand and fight, a phalanx was still the most effective way to deploy infantry in battle.

Modern armies talk of winning or losing ground, but for the phalanxes of earlier times the ground is merely the stage across which the formations move. It is the formations themselves that count, but the strength of the formation vanishes if gaps open up in the line, or if the terrain (or panic) causes the men in the formation to crowd together so closely that they cannot swing or hurl or jab with their weapons. Most of the endless drill goes into training the soldiers to maintain that vital three-foot interval—but if they are well trained, these soldiers are a formidable fighting machine.

A Greek phalanx of the fifth century BCE consisted of thousands of hoplites (heavy infantry) in serried ranks, almost fully protected in front by large shields and bronze greaves on their shins, with sixteen-foot spears extending forward beyond the shield wall. It took much time and effort to array such huge formations on a battlefield facing the enemy, and battle could not be joined at all unless the commander of the opposing phalanx cooperated. However, both sides usually wanted a prompt and decisive outcome, because the hoplites were property-owning citizens who paid for their own weapons and armor, and most of them were farmers whose crops would rot unharvested in the fields if too much time was spent on maneuver. They wanted a decision now, and generally they got it.

Fighting hoplites as depicted on a c. 5th-century BCE urn

There were tactical choices to be made beforehand: Should we make the phalanx as deep as possible to avoid being broken through, or make it shallower but longer, so as to extend past the ends of the enemy's phalanx and outflank it? But once the two phalanxes made contact, there was little more that the commanders could do.

The men in the front ranks fought each other for a time, being replaced from behind as they fell, until one side thought it was getting the upper hand. At that point, all the ranks united their efforts in a gigantic shove to break the enemy's line, and if they succeeded, then they had won. The enemy's formation would crumble, men would turn to flee, and the massacre would begin. Typically the pursuit would relent after a short while in wars between Greeks, and death on the losing side would be held to around 15 percent of the total force. In wars against non-Greeks, however, there was no quarter and no relenting in the pursuit.

> The Athenian troops weakened their center by the effort to extend the line sufficiently to cover the whole Persian front: the two wings were strong, but the line in the center was only a few ranks deep . . . The word was given to move, and the Athenians advanced at a run towards the enemy, not less than a mile away . . . the first Greeks, as far as I know, to charge at a run . . . In the center . . . the foreigners breached the Greek line . . . but the Athenians on one wing and the Plataeans on the other were both victorious . . . Then . . . they turned their attention to the Persians who had broken through in the center. Here again they were triumphant, chasing the routed enemy, and cutting them down until they came to the sea.
>
> Herodotus, describing the battle of Marathon[6]

These clumsy and bloody shoving matches like gigantic, regimented caricatures of an American football game, fought over a couple of hours on a patch of ground perhaps a hundred acres in area, could determine the future of whole peoples. There were cavalry present too, but they would almost never charge well-trained infantry who were prepared to receive them. A mass of horsemen thundering down on a formation of infantrymen may look irresistible, but horses will not run straight into an unwavering line of spear-points. They will stop or turn aside at the last moment, and as long as the infantry don't panic, they are relatively safe from charges. The cavalry's main purposes were scouting, skirmishing, and above all, riding down and killing the men of the defeated side once they had turned to flee.

Heavy infantry dominated the battlefields almost everywhere in classical times (c. 550 BCE–350 CE), and their numbers were generally less important than their discipline and morale. When Alexander the Great fought the Persian army of Darius at Issus in 333 BCE he had only forty thousand men against one hundred thousand, but his veteran hoplites charged straight across the field at the Persian center. It's just physics: forty thousand heavily armed and armored men running (slowly) in tight formation would have hit the Persian line with a force equivalent to twenty-five hundred tons moving at six or seven miles an hour, building up over just a few seconds—and at its leading edge was a hedge of spear-points. Not many men in the two front ranks of Alexander's phalanx would have survived the impact (veterans had no doubt placed themselves a little further back), but the sheer momentum of this force smashed through the center of Darius's army in only a minute or two. With the Persian army's cohesion gone, its scattered and bewildered soldiers were easy prey for Alexander's troops; probably half the Persian force was killed within two hours.

Various improvements were added to this basic formula for military success over succeeding centuries, particularly by the Romans. In two centuries of almost constant war in which they first subjugated all the other city-states of Italy and then conquered the other great power of the time, Carthage, they developed a far more flexible version of the phalanx. Roman legions were broken up into mini-phalanxes ("maniples," or handfuls) of about 150 men in three ranks, with the maniples arrayed checkerboard fashion in three overlapping lines, which gave them much greater maneuverability on broken ground. At the battle of Zama (202 BCE), where the Carthaginians tried to rout the Roman legions by a massive elephant charge, Scipio Africanus just moved the maniples of his middle line sideways in order to create straight corridors through all three lines of his formation, down which Hannibal's elephants were herded quite harmlessly.

Roman infantry face the war machines of Carthage at the Battle of Zama in 202 BCE

The weapons were modified too, partly for psychological effect. In the Roman legions the cumbersome sixteen-foot spear gave way to two throwing spears, one lighter and of longer range than the other, which the legionaries threw in succession as they advanced, plus a short sword for close-in work when they had made physical contact with the enemy. A *short* sword: get in there and do the killing in a highly personal way, because that is what really terrifies the enemy.

By high Roman times, battles had become less of a shoving match and all manner of tactical stratagems flourished, but the basic logic of the battlefield was unchanged. Men armed only with edged weapons powered by their own muscles have very limited options for effective fighting, and infantry ruled the battlefields of the third century CE as confidently as it had the battlefields of the twenty-third century BCE.

Navies

> Straightaway ship struck ship with brazen beak. The attack was started by a Greek ship which sheared off the whole prow of her Phoenician foe, and others aimed their onslaught on different opponents. At first the flood-tide of the Persian fleet held its own. But when the ships became jammed and crushed in one place, they could bring no help to each other. Ships began to strike their own friends with their bronze-jawed rams, and to shatter the whole bank of oars. The Greek ships, in careful plan, began to press round us in a circle, and ship's hulls gave in. You could no longer see the water, so full was it of wrecked vessels and dead men, while the beaches and rocks were thick with corpses.
>
> Aeschylus, describing the battle of Salamis (from the Persian point of view) in *The Persians*, 472 BCE[7]

Nobody needed navies until civilizations began to produce goods like grain, wine, minerals, and timber that were worth trading in bulk. Most of that trade was conducted by sea (it still is), and attacking the commercial ships of wealthy states became an obvious and highly profitable strategy in war. Moving whole armies by sea was also an attractive military option in the Mediterranean, where the sea was generally the quickest route between any two points. Large fleets of warships soon came to dominate naval conflict in the Mediterranean. Their first purpose was to eliminate the other side's navy, after which the defenseless merchant ships could be plundered with impunity.

Like many artifacts of the classical world, the war galley rapidly matured into a standard design, whose technology then scarcely changed for several thousand years. Merchant ships used a combination of sail and oars, but warships, which needed to move rapidly in any direction regardless of wind, depended mainly on muscle power: up to several hundred rowers to pull the naval vessels through the water at high speed.

Artist's rendition of a 4th-century BCE trireme

A ship is a kind of machine, and making big machines in large numbers called for techniques of organization and production resembling those of industrial societies. When Greece was faced with the great Persian invasion early in the fifth century BCE, the Athenian shipyards adopted mass production methods, producing between six and eight triremes (galleys with three banks of oars) each month for over two years. They were paid for with the accumulated silver reserves of the state. By 480 BCE some 250 galleys had been built, requiring over forty thousand men to crew them. All the military manpower of Athens went into the fleet, leaving the other Greek city-states to provide the land forces for the peninsula's defense. And it was the Greek fleet, predominantly Athenian, that destroyed the Persian fleet at Salamis and forced the emperor Xerxes to retreat from Greece.

Naval warfare in classical times was a simple affair. Two fleets of galleys, which might number in the hundreds, would line up facing each other off some stretch of coastline, and charge. The ships would try to hole each other head-on with their bronze rams, or at least shear off the oars on one side of the enemy galley (crushing most of the rowers in the process) then turn back and ram the disabled enemy from astern. Often, however, they would end up lying alongside each other, with the soldiers on each galley fighting it out along the decks of one ship or the other, as in the battle in Syracuse harbor in 413 BCE, where almost two hundred ships fought one another in a very confined space.

> Many ships crowded in upon each other in a small area. Consequently there were not many attacks made with the rams amidships . . . Once the ships met, the soldiers fought hand to hand, each trying to board the enemy. Because of the narrowness of the space, it often happened that . . . three or more ships found themselves jammed together, so that the steersmen had to think of defense on one side and attack on the other . . . and the great din of all these ships crashing together was not only frightening in itself, but also made it impossible to hear the orders given by the boat swains.
>
> Thucydides, *History of the Peloponnesian Wars*[8]

The greatest naval battles of classical times were fought between Rome, essentially a land power at the beginning of the Punic wars in 264 BCE, and Carthage, a maritime power with allies or possessions in Spain, Sardinia, Sicily, and southern Italy. The naval harbor of Carthage (near modern Tunis) was a man-made circular space over a thousand yards across, with a central island and sheds for working on two hundred galleys at once—and it could turn out as many as sixty galleys a month.

In the generations of war that convulsed the western Mediterranean between 264 and 146 BCE, the Romans also learned to build and fight a navy. In the naval battles that followed, and even more so in the sudden storms that sometimes overtook the fleets of flimsy galleys in open waters, the casualties were huge.

At Ecnomus off the coast of North Africa in 256 BCE, a Roman fleet of 330 galleys routed a Carthaginian fleet of equal size, sinking thirty ships and capturing sixty-four, a loss to the Carthaginians of between thirty and forty thousand men. On its return to Italy, the Roman fleet was caught in a great storm off the west coast of Sicily, and 270 of its galleys were sunk or driven ashore, drowning about a hundred thousand men. Never since has there been so great a loss of life in naval warfare.

Eighteen hundred years after Ecnomus, in 1571 CE, the allied naval forces of western Europe fought the Turkish navy at Lepanto. There were over two hundred galleys on each side, built according to designs that would have caused no surprise in the shipyards of ancient Carthage. The tactics would have been equally familiar: ram if you can, board if you can't. Thirty thousand men drowned in that one afternoon.

> *Carthago delenda est.*
> (Carthage must be destroyed.)
>
> Cato the Elder

A society that can send a hundred thousand men to sea would be a formidable contender in the great-power stakes even today, and Rome and Carthage were not just building huge fleets of warships. At times they were also maintaining armies on three or four fronts simultaneously, spread all over the western Mediterranean. At the height of the Second Punic War in 213 BCE, 29 percent of Rome's male citizens were serving in the army,[9] a level that was rarely exceeded even in the great wars of the last century—and although Rome was ultimately victorious, 10 percent of its entire male population was killed in battle during the final two decades of the war.[10] As for the Carthaginians, their casualties were virtually total: not even their language survived. Even so, these two powers were not really waging "total war" in the modern sense of the word.

Rome was a complex and sophisticated civilization, but its interest in technological innovation was very low* and it lacked the wealth necessary for genuine total war. The city-states of Rome and Carthage, each with fewer than a million full citizens, mobilized a high proportion of their own populations, but only a tiny fraction of the other people throughout the large empires they controlled. The basic military equation of premodern times held true: societies whose economic base is

---

* Between Lepanto and the first moon landing (398 years) Western civilization went from galleys to spaceships. In the 580 years between the battles of Ecnomus and the Hellespont, the last major engagement of the Roman Navy, Roman galley design hardly changed at all.

subsistence agriculture cannot afford to withdraw more than around 3 percent of their population from food production in order to send them off to war.

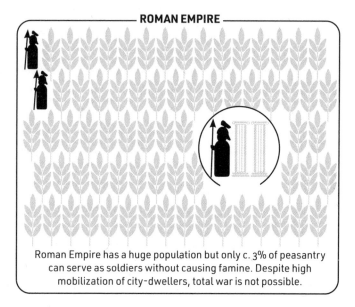

— **ROMAN EMPIRE** —

Roman Empire has a huge population but only c. 3% of peasantry can serve as soldiers without causing famine. Despite high mobilization of city-dwellers, total war is not possible.

The size of the Roman army a few centuries later, when Rome ruled the entire Mediterranean and had legions guarding borders as far away as Scotland and Sudan, is a fair measure of the maximum size of military forces that a premodern agrarian society—even one with highly developed commerce—could sustain over the long run. Even in the late third century CE, when the empire's population had risen to one hundred million and the barbarian pressure on the frontiers was getting serious, the Roman army never exceeded three quarters of a million troops.[11]

It was a very good army, and quite modern in many respects. The troops were reasonably well paid, they were well trained, and they could even expect a decent pension if they lived long enough to retire. In the centurions, it had the first professional officer corps. Against other civilized armies it was almost guaranteed to win in the long run—and it hadn't really had to fight against the horse nomads, because the civilized world of Europe and the Middle East had not had to contend with any major barbarian invasions for almost a thousand years. But then some change in climate or population out on the Central Asian steppes set the nomads moving again, and a few generations later the ripple effect began to hit the borders of the Roman empire. In the end, the empire went under, and most of Europe's civilization with it. It was almost a thousand years before it regained its former level.

Western Darkness, Eastern Light

The classical world took a long time dying. Western Europe was overrun by the Germanic invasions in the fourth and fifth centuries, but virtually the whole of the Eastern Roman Empire survived intact for another two hundred years. Arabs united by the new faith of Islam conquered North Africa and the Fertile Crescent in the seventh and eighth centuries, but a Greek-speaking and Christianized version of Roman civilization (Byzantium) survived in the Balkans and Asia Minor until incoming Turkish nomads destroyed the main Byzantine army at Manzikert in 1071. But both the Arabs and the Turks were relatively small groups of conquerors ruling over larger and more sophisticated populations, and what emerged under their rule was an Islamized version of classical civilization, preserving and even refining the urban, literate, and commercial character of that culture.

In western Europe, however, the invaders were whole societies on the move who shared few of the assumptions and values of the civilized peoples they conquered. They came with an elite of mounted warriors, but the great majority were subsistence farmers from beyond the borders of the Roman empire, partly drawn by the prospect of loot, partly fleeing before horse nomads from the steppes like the Huns. When they arrived in present-day France or Spain or Italy, they mostly settled down to farm again. They never outnumbered the surviving Roman citizens in the western parts of the empire, and the fact that they were soon Christianized helped to ensure that it was the Latin language of the conquered, not their own Germanic tongues, which ended up as the common language in most places. But there were enough of these newcomers to ensure that it was their way of running things that prevailed, not the old ways evolved during three thousand years of imperial rule in the Middle Eastern/Mediterranean world. In the west, classical civilization actually died.

EUROPE
AFTER THE FALL OF ROME

THE WEST	THE EAST
Latin-speaking, Roman Catholic	Greek-speaking, Orthodox Christian
is occupied by entire societies from Germanic lands	is conquered by small Arab or Turkish military elite
...who adopt Christianity and late Latin but retain their own nonclassical culture.	...who adopt Islamized version of existing classical culture. Greek eventually supplanted by Arabic or Turkish.

Horses Come Back

When a stable social structure reemerged in western Europe after several centuries of almost total breakdown, it was based on an extreme dispersion of political and military power. The real power base in feudal times was not the state (which scarcely existed), but the few dozens or hundreds of square miles either granted to some local warrior or just seized by him. The only military tool available to what passed for a central administration in the kingdom was an assembly of such landed warriors—if they decided to show up—for as long as they were willing to stay. And cavalry came to dominate the battlefield both in the east and in the west.

14th-century miniature of a cavalry clash during the Second Crusade, from William of Tyre's *Histoire d'Outremer*

In the Muslim east, warfare until the fifteenth century remained fully in the nomad tradition: fast, lightly armed, and armored clouds of horsemen who used composite bows for harassing attacks from a safe distance, and the sword and light lance for the much rarer occasions when they took on their opponents at close quarters. In the west, however, cavalry warfare gradually evolved into the unique form of heavily armored riders, astride lumbering horses bred for their ability to bear weight, relying on the sheer physical impact of their charge.

By the time of the Crusades in the twelfth century the cavalry of Christendom were fighting like a mounted phalanx—a heavily armored phalanx eight feet tall and moving at twenty-five miles an hour. If it hit you, that was the end of it, but it was pretty easy to evade the Crusaders' charge if you were not culturally committed to fighting that way (which is why the Christian armies had to go back home to Europe in the end). And by the late Middle Ages, when the population, prosperity and organizational competence of western Europe were again approaching the levels of Roman times, infantry reemerged as the dominant force on the battlefield, even though there had been no significant change in the technology of weapons.

CHAPTER 5

Absolute Monarchs and Limited War
1400–1790

Infantry Comes Back

Infantry weapons began their comeback on the battlefield in the latter stage of the Hundred Years' War (early fifteenth century), when English longbowmen dug outward-pointing stakes into the ground to protect themselves from charging horses and repeatedly decimated French formations of heavily armored cavalry.

The arrows from the longbows (and the new crossbows) could penetrate chain mail at a considerable distance, so the mounted knights were forced to use plate armor carefully designed with ridges and oblique facets that would deflect arrows, but they couldn't protect their horses with similar armor. The weight was simply too great. In the last battles of the Hundred Years' War, like Agincourt in 1415, dismounted French knights wearing about sixty pounds of plate armor charged on foot; or rather, they died trying.

The lesson was learned: what we need is real infantry, not dismounted horsemen in metal clothing. By the sixteenth century, combat once again centered on clashes of heavy infantry, fighting in a style that would have been familiar to Alexander the Great. He could have taken command of either side when two armies clashed at Ceresole, not far from Turin, toward the end of the Italian wars in 1544—as long as he'd learned the right languages, and taken a short course on firearms.

Now with Guns

The infantry phalanxes were essentially the same, carrying pikes that were no more than glorified spears, but the French side placed a rank of *arquebusiers* (men armed with heavy matchlock muskets that fired a half-ounce bullet) behind the first rank of pikemen. As Captain Blaise de Montluc explained:

> In this way we should kill all their captains in the front rank. But we found they were as ingenious as ourselves, for behind their first line of pikes they had put pistoleers. Neither side fired till we were touching—and then there was wholesale slaughter. Every shot told: the front rank on each side went down. The second and third ranks met over the corpses of their comrades in front, the rear ranks pushing them forward. And as we pushed harder, the enemy tumbled over.[1]

16th-century musket-wielding infantry on the march during the Italian wars

Despite the firearms, it was still basically the same old shoving match: the "push of pike," as men of the sixteenth century called it. The French and their Swiss mercenary allies had the advantage of pushing downhill, and when French cavalry hit their German infanty opponents, the *Landsknechte*, in the flank, their formation folded up, and they were herded into a tightly packed mob where they had no space to use their pikes. Out of seven thousand *Landsknechte*, nearly five thousand were slaughtered. The Italian infantry on the left of the line had already marched off the field to save itself, but when the Spanish veterans on the Imperial right tried to retreat through a small wood in their rear, they were quickly cut off by the French cavalry, with the French infantry close behind.

> And when they descried us only 400 paces away, and with our cavalry ready to charge, they threw down their pikes and surrendered to the horsemen. You might see fifteen or twenty of them around a man at arms, pressing about him and asking for quarter, for fear of us of the infantry who were wanting to cut all their throats. A great many—perhaps half—got killed, the rest were accepted as prisoners.
>
> Blaise de Montluc[2]

It was full circle: what happened at Ceresole was indistinguishable, except in minor details, from what had happened under the walls of Umma four thousand years before, or at Issus halfway between the two.

The Age of Mercenaries

> Blessed be those happy ages that were strangers to the dreadful fury of these devilish instruments of artillery, whose inventor I am satisfied is now in hell, receiving the reward of his cursed invention, which is the cause that very often a cowardly base hand takes away the life of the bravest gentleman.
>
> Miguel de Cervantes, *Don Quixote*

In the sixteenth century the most powerful weapons in the world, the great siege cannons, were capable of killing perhaps half a dozen people (if they stood close together) at a range of a few hundred yards. Today, less than five centuries later, the modern counterparts of those weapons, the intercontinental ballistic missiles, can kill several million people at a range of seven or eight thousand miles. But only the very last phase of the process that delivered us from there to here was dominated by technology.

Until the last 150 years, the weapons used by the West were nothing special. Indeed, the so-called gunpowder empires of the Islamic world, Ottoman, Safavid (Persian), and Moghul, were quicker off the mark with firearms, making both arquebuses and cannon central to their battle tactics at an earlier date: the first standing infantry force equipped with firearms in the world was the Janissaries of Mehmed II's Ottoman army in the 1440s.[3]

What happened in fifteenth- and sixteenth-century Europe was the creation of modern centralized states by ambitious monarchs who sought absolute power. To succeed they had to destroy the military power of the old feudal aristocracy, which was mainly based on providing the kingdom with cavalry. The solution was to reinvent the classical armies of antiquity, which were more effective in combat. More importantly, the nobility, who had hitherto been able to blackmail the king by threatening not to fight or provide horsepower in times of war, now lost a vital instrument of leverage. The switch to infantry was very much in the monarch's political interest.

On the other hand, the monarchs were not interested in arming their ordinary subjects and giving them military training. The subjects might then use their new skills and their numbers to challenge the monarchs' absolute power. So the kings and queens chose instead to hire mercenaries who sold their loyalty to any government willing to pay them. In the poorer parts of Europe like Switzerland, exporting companies of trained mercenary soldiers became a national industry[4]— and because mercenaries cost so much, armies stayed small. The average sixteenth-century battle involved only about ten thousand men per side.

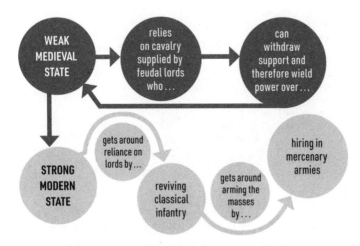

Armies all over Europe followed the model adopted by the Spaniards, the most successful military power of the age, right down to the early seventeenth century. They had solid *tercios* (phalanxes) of pikemen, sixteen, twenty, or even thirty ranks deep. There were musketeers at the corners of the formation and heavy, barely mobile field artillery across the front of the line, but gunpowder weapons played a distinctly secondary role.

Even these cumbersome firearms, however, were more effective than those in China, where the explosive results of mixing saltpeter, sulfur, and charcoal had first been discovered. As early as 1232, Chinese troops defending the city of Luoyang against the Mongols had used a "thunder bomb," an iron vessel filled with gunpowder and launched from a catapult. Within twenty-five years, they were using the "fire lance," a primitive gun consisting of a bamboo tube stuffed with gunpowder that would fire a cluster of pellets about 250 yards. It was probably Mongol armies, having copied the Chinese weapons, who brought them to Europe, where the first real metal guns were cast in the 1320s.[5]

Thunder bombs away: earliest known image of a Chinese fire lance

Why China never developed firearms any further is a major historical puzzle, for the country's other technologies, from printing to seagoing ships, remained abreast or ahead of European technologies as late as 1500. It may just be that China's main adversaries, the Mongols and other pastoral peoples, did not push the technology any further themselves (pastoralists tend not to). At any rate, China never independently went beyond fire lances, while both in Europe and in the Muslim empires firearms developed within two centuries into giant cannons able to hurl an iron shot weighing 1,125 pounds at city walls, and into portable arquebuses (early muskets) firing half-ounce bullets to an effective range of one hundred yards.

These new firearms had a bigger role in sieges than in battles, and more at sea than on land. It was the Turkish army's massed cannons that breached the walls of Constantinople, for most of the previous millennium the world's greatest city, in 1453: they just banged away and dug a deeper and deeper groove at the base of the walls until they fell under their own weight. At sea the broad-beamed, oceangoing sailing ships of western Europe proved to be ideal artillery platforms. By the early 1500s the cannons were mounted to fire broadsides at close range, and artillery duels between cannons ranged on two or even three decks would decide most battles at sea for the next three hundred years. On the battlefield itself, however, gunpowder weapons took much longer to come into their own.

Early firearms like arquebuses had the same range as cross-bows, took less training to use, and they made a satisfactory bang, but the arquebusiers remained a secondary element in battle up to the seventeenth century. The core of the army was still the massed ranks of disciplined pikemen who could defend themselves (and the arquebusiers) from cavalry charges, and whose clashes with the other side's similarly equipped pha-lanxes of pikemen were generally decisive.

But this unwieldy, slowed-down version of classical warfare was to change in the cataclysm known as the Thirty Years' War.

Thirty Years, Eight Million Dead

From the mid-sixteenth century the Protestant Reformation set off local religious wars in Europe like a string of firecrackers— notably ten civil wars in France that killed an estimated three million people in 1562–98, and an eighty-year uprising against Spanish rule in the Netherlands beginning in 1568. In the years after 1618, however, these local quarrels merged into the first war in which all the European powers were involved. By the time the Thirty Years' War ended in 1648, battles had assumed the form they would retain until little more than a century ago, and eight million people were dead.

The religious passions were real, but it was governments, not churches, that fought the war. Unintended but inevitable, a unified system of European states was emerging, in which everybody was playing in the same continent-wide game: a balance-of-power system where every increase in might for one state was automatically a loss of security for all the others. Countries as far apart as Sweden and Spain, with no concrete reasons for fighting each other, ended up killing each other's troops on the battlefields of Germany—and in the end, religion was less important than the zero-sum game of power. That is why, toward the end of the war, when the Catholic Hapsburg dynasty (Spain and Austria) seemed to be getting too strong, Catholic France allied itself with the weakening Protestant powers and prolonged the war until the "balance of power" was restored.

It was Germany, where most of the battles of the Thirty Years' War were fought, that paid the price for this policy.

Drunk with victory, the troops defied all efforts to control them ... Towards midday flames suddenly shot up at almost the same moment at twenty different places. There was no time for (generals) Tilly and Pappenheim to ask whence came the fire; staring in consternation, they rallied the drunken, disorderly, exhausted men to fight it. The wind was too strong, and in a few minutes the city was a furnace, the wooden houses crashing to their foundations in columns of smoke and flame. The cry was now to save the army and the imperialist officers struggled in vain to drive their men into the open. Rapidly whole quarters were cut off by walls of smoke so that those who lingered for booty or lost their way, or lay in a drunken stupor in the cellars, alike perished.

C. V. Wedgwood, *The Thirty Years' War*[6]

Tilly's entry into the destroyed city of Magdeburg, May 25, 1631

Magdeburg's sack and destruction in 1631, with the death of some forty thousand inhabitants, was just another incident in a seemingly endless war. Mercenary armies marched across Germany season after season, spreading disease in their wake. Starving groups of refugees and lawless bands of deserters roamed the countryside, stealing food from the peasants who were still working their land. There were cases of cannibalism. By the time the Peace of Westphalia ended the slaughter in 1648, Germany's population had fallen by over one third: from twenty-one million to only thirteen million.

Then, quite abruptly, the steady escalation in the scale of European wars stopped. No subsequent war in Europe caused deaths on anything like the same scale until the early nineteenth century, and civilian losses never outnumbered military casualties again until the mid-twentieth century. But the new restraint shown by Europe's rulers after 1648 was not a response to the huge casualty toll. The overwhelming majority of the war's victims had been German peasants, about whom nobody powerful really cared. The 350,000 soldiers killed were a bigger concern, for they were very expensive to train and maintain. But what really persuaded the surviving rulers to impose limits on their future wars was the painfully learned lesson that if war got too badly out of hand, whole states and dynasties could disappear (as many did during the Thirty Years' War).

The primary goal of any dynasty is survival, and the Thirty Years' War taught the monarchs who survived that they had to cooperate—at least a little bit. They could fight wars against each other, seize border provinces and overseas colonies, undermine and betray each other to their hearts' content, but no member of the rulers' club would ever again be allowed to lose so badly as to disappear from the game entirely (except Poland, which was partitioned by the unanimous agreement of all its powerful neighbors.) An age of far more limited warfare was coming.

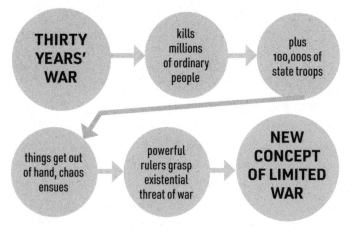

Swedish Innovation

Firearms finally took over the battlefield during the Thirty Years' War, but this wasn't due to any great improvement in the weapons. It was the tactics that changed, and the man responsible was King Gustavus Adolphus of Sweden. His kingdom had only a million and a half people, leaving it at a permanent disadvantage against the stronger surrounding countries, so he tried to compensate by changing the way the weapons were used. In doing so, he created the first army that Alexander the Great would not have known how to command.

Solid formations of pikemen standing shoulder to shoulder still ruled the battlefields of Europe, but Gustavus Adolphus realized that they were ideal targets for gunfire, if you could concentrate enough of it onto them. No doubt others had the same insight, but they lacked either the courage or the authority to make the radical tactical changes needed to take advantage.

Gustavus Adolphus had both, so he turned two-thirds of his pikemen into musketeers, ranged in ranks only three deep and trained to fire in volleys (one line standing, one crouching, and one kneeling). He also dumped the cumbersome field artillery that needed twenty-four horses to move it, and substituted lighter guns that could be pulled by only one or two horses and used a prepared cartridge—so they could be moved around the battlefield much faster, even under fire, and they fired far more often.

The Swedish king's army could shatter a formation of pikemen from a hundred yards away with no need for physical contact; just musket volleys and cannon fire. Then, once the bullets and cannonballs had torn enough holes in the enemy's formation, his cavalry would charge and turn disorder into rout.

When the Swedes arrived in Germany in 1630 to rescue the failing Protestant cause, they easily demolished the old-style armies of their "imperial" (i.e., Spanish and Austrian) opponents. Gustavus Adophus himself was killed in battle in 1632, and in the end the Swedish intervention there was not decisive—but every other army in Europe rapidly adopted the revolutionary tactics originated by the Swedish king.

Drill

Firearms and not cold steel now decide battles.

J. F. Puysegur, 1748[7]

By 1700, pikemen had disappeared and all infantrymen carried flintlock muskets, much improved firearms that could be loaded and fired twice a minute. The muskets were inaccurate even at a hundred yards, but that was not a problem because they were not intended for use against individual targets. An infantry battalion's job was only to deliver volleys of fire. It was a sort of human machine gun with several hundred moving parts (the soldiers), able to deliver a single burst of fire every thirty seconds.

During the battle of Fontenoy in 1745, the British Guards Brigade, emerging from a sunken road, found itself only a couple of hundred yards from a large formation of French infantry. The French officers invited the British commander, Lord Charles Hay, to open fire, but he replied: "No, sir, we never fire first. After you," and continued to advance until the French finally let off their volley. While they reloaded, the surviving British troops marched on to a distance of only thirty paces and fired an answering volley that killed or wounded nineteen officers and six hundred men of the French regiment in a single second—whereupon the rest broke and fled. The famous command given to the American revolutionary troops at Bunker Hill—"Hold your fire until you see the whites of their eyes"—was not bravado. It was the standard tactical doctrine of the time.

The job of a private soldier in an eighteenth-century battle was essentially to carry out the several dozen complicated movements necessary to load and aim his musket while facing what amounted to a firing squad only a hundred yards away. To get men to do this took years of training and utterly ruthless discipline: Prussian army regulations stated that "if a soldier during an action looks as if about to flee, or so much as sets foot outside the line, the non-commissioned officer standing behind him will run him through with his bayonet and kill him on the spot."[8]

Musket drill from *L'Art Militaire pour l'Infanterie* by von Wallhausen, 1630

"It never entered my mind that we were at war"

The casualties in an eighteenth-century battle rivaled anything in ancient warfare: at Blenheim in 1704 the victors lost 12,500 men (24 percent of their force), and the losers suffered 20,000 killed and wounded (40 percent of their force) in five hours of fighting on a single day. During the Seven Years' War (1756–63) the Prussian army lost 180,000 dead, three times the number it started out with.[9] And yet the century and a half between the Thirty Years' War and the French Revolution (1648–1789) truly was an era of limited war.

The actual battles got bigger—from an average of ten thousand men to thirty thousand soldiers on each side in the course of the Thirty Years' War, and up again to the hundred thousand mark in the biggest battles of the eighteenth century—but their political and economic impact on civilian society was very small. Some distant territory might change hands or a different candidate might gain a throne somewhere, but population, prosperity, and industry continued to grow across most of Europe and the wars barely registered in the consciousness of the average civilian. At the height of the Seven Years' War (1756–63), the Anglo-Irish novelist Laurence Sterne left London for Paris without getting the necessary passport to travel in an enemy country ("it never entered my mind that we were at war with France"), but nobody stopped him at the French coast, and the French foreign minister courteously sent him a passport after he had arrived at Versailles.[10]

Nobles and Vagabonds

By 1700, almost every kingdom of Europe had created a standing army made up of "regular" soldiers paid directly by the government. Unlike mercenaries, regular troops had to be paid even in peacetime, but they were more reliable and they freed the monarchs from having to rely on ordinary citizens for military help in a crisis. Instead, the armies of Europe ended up being composed almost everywhere of "nobles and vagabonds."

The newly centralized monarchies bought off the old aristocratic class by giving them a monopoly on officers' jobs in the new regular armies: they were losing their real power as the source of wealth shifted steadily from land to trade, but they got to keep their prestige. Their soldiers came from the other extreme of the social spectrum: the best were landless peasants; the worst were drunks and outright criminals. It was generally believed that keeping control of such men required the regular use of the lash and the hangman's noose: "In general, the common soldier must fear his officers more than the enemy," said Frederick the Great,[11] and Wellington remarked of his troops: "I don't know if they frighten the enemy; but by God they frighten me!" Yet the trained soldier, though despised as an individual, was an expensive commodity whose life the state was reluctant to squander in battle.

Limitations

Countries fought their wars mainly with the troops they had available at the start, since it took several years of repetitive training accompanied by physical violence as punishment for the slightest error, to instill the complex drills and instant, blind obedience that would make their soldiers useful in battle. That meant the armies had to be kept up to full strength even in peacetime, which added to the expense. And the soldiers were still likely to desert, especially if battle seemed imminent.

European armies of this era could not "live off the land": if the soldiers were allowed to forage for themselves, the army would simply melt away. So there had to be some central magazine near the area of operations, prepared long beforehand, which stored huge amounts of food for the troops. The field ovens could advance up to sixty miles from the magazine in order to bake the bread, and the bread wagons could deliver it another forty miles to the army, but that was the limit. In theory, no army could advance more than a hundred miles into enemy territory without setting up an intermediate magazine. Despite the tight control under which they were kept (and the meticulous catering arrangements) eighty thousand men managed to desert from the Russian army during the Seven Years' War, and seventy thousand from the French.[12]

The Duke of Marlborough's siege train at the Battle of Schellenberg, 1704

Moreover, armies could only campaign when there was grass in the fields (May to October), because an army of a hundred thousand men was typically accompanied by forty thousand animals. Those forty thousand animals went through eight hundred acres of grass a day, so armies spent much of their time just moving to new grazing grounds.[13] Wars were therefore fought mostly in well-defined border areas that were full of fortresses, and consisted mainly of sieges. In 1708, Marlborough's siege train of eighteen heavy guns and twenty siege mortars required three thousand wagons and sixteen thousand horses to move it and took thirty miles of road. Armies maneuvered to threaten each other's supply lines and force a withdrawal, but actual battles were relatively rare because soldiers were too expensive to waste. As France's Marshal Saxe remarked in 1732: "I do not favor pitched battles . . . and I am convinced that a skilful general could make war all his life without being forced into one."[14]

All these practical limitations on war were reinforced by the fact that the players were living in a balance-of-power system: no great power could suffer total defeat, because the others would pile in to stop the big winner from taking over the whole system. The downside of this system, however, is that it draws every major power into any war involving the biggest players: it becomes a "world war." The term is relatively new, but the concept is not. For over 350 years, ever since the Thirty Years' War, almost every one of Europe's major wars, whatever its specific origin, has rapidly spread to involve all the great powers of the time.

THIRTY YEARS' WAR → age of limited war under balance-of-power system → bilateral conflicts tend to widen into multi-lateral conflicts, or "world wars"

By the eighteenth century, with European empires running most of the rest of the planet as well, they were also world wars in the purely geographical sense. During the Seven Years' War, for example, not only were the European powers of France, Austria, Sweden, and Russia ranged against Great Britain, Prussia, and Hanover, but there was also fighting on every continent except Australia. In the peace settlement, Britain, the biggest winner, gained Canada, Senegal, and some West Indies. It also retained most of the fruits of Clive's military victories in India, but had to return Cuba, the Philippines, and Argentina to Spain. The only respects in which the Seven Years' War didn't match the modern definition of a world war were the lethality of the killing systems and the scale of the casualties.

Europe did "conquer the world," so to speak, but it happened in two different phases, and the first was dead easy. The European conquest of the Stone Age peoples of the Americas in the sixteenth and seventeenth centuries did not require technology and organization of a very high order. The array of quick-killer epidemic diseases, evolved over ten thousand years in the crowded cities of Eurasia, devastated the native populations even before a shot was fired. The human population of the Americas dropped by at least 90 percent in the course of the 1500s due to epidemic diseases, and when the forests reclaimed their abandoned farms (the native peoples were almost all farmers), the new trees extracted so much carbon dioxide from the atmosphere that it helped to trigger the "Little Ice Age."[15]

The actual conquests still required military violence, of course, but the Europeans' horses and their iron weapons over-awed the natives, and the methodical Eurasian ruthlessness of the invaders shocked them into passivity. However, any other civilized domain—the Ottoman Empire in the Middle East, the Moghul Empire in India, or the Chinese Empire—could have subjugated the peoples of the Americas just as easily, had they possessed the oceangoing ships and the commercial drive to take them there. On land, the Muslim world was certainly powerful enough: its armies were still roughly comparable to those of Christian Europe, and as late as 1683 an Ottoman army was able to besiege Vienna, more than halfway from Istanbul to Paris.

At that point, European power in other parts of Eurasia, and even in Africa, rarely extended inland beyond the range of a cannon shot: their ships were unbeatable, but their armies were less so. The second phase of the conquest (1700–1900), when the British conquered most of India, the Ottoman borders began to contract under Austrian and Russian pressure, and Africa was finally brought under colonial rule, was militarily more demanding, and only at the very end of that period did European weapons technology make any significant advances. But the rigid discipline and ruthlessly efficient organization that the Europeans brought to the use of these weapons, backed by their rapidly growing wealth, could not be matched by their opponents elsewhere.

To a European of the last generation before the French Revolution, therefore, war would have seemed at worst a bearable evil. One by one the other parts of the Old World were falling under European rule, while in Europe itself cities were not sacked, civilians did not face intolerable demands for their taxes and their sons in order to fight wars, and whole countries did not disappear or dissolve into chaos as a result of war. The institution of war had been brought under control, limited and rationalized (as that extremely rational age might have put it).

But in the eighteenth century, few realized how fragile all these limitations were.

CHAPTER 6

Mass Warfare

1790–1900

Revolution

The balance of power will continue to fluctuate, and the prosperity of our own or the neighboring kingdoms may be alternately exalted and depressed; but these partial events cannot essentially injure our general state of happiness . . . In peace, the progress of knowledge and industry is accelerated by the emulation of so many active rivals; in war, the European forces are exercised by temperate and undecisive contests.

Edward Gibbon, 1782[1]

From this moment until that in which our enemies shall have been driven from the territory of the Republic, all Frenchmen are permanently requisitioned for service in the armies. The young men shall fight; the married men shall forge weapons and transport supplies; the women will make tents and clothes and serve in hospitals . . . The public buildings shall be turned into barracks, the public squares into munition factories . . . All firearms of suitable calibre shall be turned over to the troops . . . All saddle horses shall be seized for the cavalry; all draft horses not employed in cultivation will draw the artillery and supply wagons.

Decree of the National Convention, Paris, 1793[2]

The idyllic world described by Gibbon had less than a decade to run when he wrote those words—and it was never that idyllic for the great majority of the population. At some level Europe's absolute monarchs understood that there was a great deal of resentment, even anger, in the "lower orders" of society, and that they should not exploit the military resources of their kingdoms to the full in war because doing so could unleash social and political forces that would threaten their thrones. Only limited wars were safe. But ideas about equality and democracy were the common currency of late eighteenth-century thought, and even as Gibbon wrote, the first revolution based on those ideas was triumphing in the new United States.

Mass Armies

In 1789 the revolution arrived in France, then by far the richest and most populous country in Europe. All the other monarchies of Europe rightly saw this as a mortal threat, and launched their armies against France to stamp out the revolution. In France, the National Convention responded by declaring conscription, and by New Year's Day 1794 the French armies numbered about 770,000 men.[3] The wars of mass armies that ensued ravaged Europe for the next two decades.

The French Revolution, with its principles of liberty and equality, first stimulated and then exploited a fervent nationalism that made conscription acceptable. The enthusiastic soldiers of the "nation in arms" had the loyalty and the initiative to fight in more open and mobile formations, and they were so numerous that they often just overwhelmed the regular troops of the old regimes.

Since the new French armies were much less likely to desert, they could live off the land: if there was no bread, they could dig in the fields for potatoes. They could therefore cut loose from the magazines and supply trains of former days and move much faster and farther: a hundred miles was no longer their maximum practical range. They could also be turned loose to pursue and destroy a retreating enemy without fear that they would all desert, so battles rarely ended in draws anymore. As Karl von Clausewitz, a Prussian officer who first saw action against the revolutionary forces at the age of twelve in 1793, put it, "the colossal weight of the whole French people, unhinged by political fanaticism, came crashing down on us."[4]

Emperor Napoleon 1 of France reviewing the Grenadiers of the Imperial Guard on June 1, 1811, in Paris

Not much was said about the democratic ideals of the revolution after Napoleon made himself emperor in 1804: the war's aim was now simply to establish French domination over all of Europe. And yet Napoleon managed to keep going for another ten years of almost constant war, feeding French nationalism on a constant diet of military victories and resorting to compulsion whenever necessary. Between 1804 and 1813, he drafted 2.4 million men into the army, fewer than half of whom returned home at the end of the empire. "Troops are made to get killed," he once said, although as time went by the conscripts became less willing. By 1810, 80 percent of the annual quota of French conscripts failed to appear voluntarily.[5]

War was still very expensive, but the highly centralized government that had been created by the revolutionary regime could get more out of the economy than the old French monarchy had ever dared to demand. The new state-owned arms factories benefited from strict controls on prices and wages. Equipment, food, and horses were simply requisitioned, with payment made later at government-set prices, or never. And in the early days, as the conquests began to accumulate, so much money was coming in from abroad that for a time the wars actually paid for themselves.

NAPOLEON'S ADVANTAGE

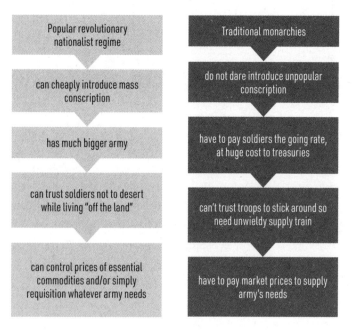

Popular revolutionary nationalist regime	Traditional monarchies
can cheaply introduce mass conscription	do not dare introduce unpopular conscription
has much bigger army	have to pay soldiers the going rate, at huge cost to treasuries
can trust soldiers not to desert while living "off the land"	can't trust troops to stick around so need unwieldy supply train
can control prices of essential commodities and/or simply requisition whatever army needs	have to pay market prices to supply army's needs

The monarchies that were fighting the French had a much harder task, because they had to match the size of the revolutionary armies but they did not dare to introduce universal conscription. They had to pay all their troops the going rate for regular soldiers, which put a huge burden on their treasuries. Indeed Britain, which had to subsidize most of the others, was obliged to introduce the world's first income tax in 1799 to meet its commitments.

It still wasn't enough: Napoleon and his marshals kept winning most of the battles—partly because he was a brilliant commander, but also because he had an almost inexhaustible supply of cannon fodder. Nor could the assorted kings, princes, and dukes save their thrones by collaborating with Napoleon. From the start the French revolutionary armies replaced monarchies with republican regimes (carefully chosen to be pro-French) in the countries they conquered. Napoleon went even further, annexing entire kingdoms or turning them into satellites with his own relatives or French field marshals as their rulers. If the monarchs of Europe wanted to keep their thrones, they would have to take the risk of arming their own people. In the end, some of them did.

Mass Media

No great technological change took place in the late eighteenth and early nineteenth centuries, and there was no sudden surge of new wealth. The smoothbore muskets carried by the infantry were the same as they had been for several generations, and so were the ships-of-the-line. The real transformation was political, not military: for the first time ever, mass societies had found a way to ditch their autocratic rulers and revive the old human principle of equality.

In less than fifteen years, popular revolutions overthrew the monarchs first in the British colonies in America (population three million), and then in France, the biggest state in Europe (population thirty million). These were the first large states whose official values were closer to those of our hunter-gatherer ancestors than to the hierarchy of the anthill. Why did it happen now, and why among the Europeans rather than in the Islamic empires or in China?

The answer is almost certainly the invention of the first mass medium: print. The printing press was originally a Chinese invention, as was movable type, but printing had a much bigger impact in Western countries for several reasons, the main one probably being differing levels of literacy. In the West, the Reformation had made paramount the individual's relationship with God, and the reading and understanding of God's word in the Bible, supercharging the drive toward literacy. Under the Ottomans and in China, however, reading and writing remained for far longer the province of a specific class. As late as 1900, only 10 percent of the Chinese population was literate; in 1935, only 15 percent of Turkish people could read. The potential audience was just not there. Whereas the male literacy rate in England in 1700 was 40 percent—and in New England it was 70 percent.[6]

There were few newspapers as yet, but books and pamphlets were everywhere. Ten million books were printed in Europe in the fifteenth century, but two hundred million in the sixteenth, half a billion in the seventeenth, and a billion in the eighteenth.[7] Tom Paine's forty-nine-page pamphlet *Common Sense*, published in 1776 in Philadelphia, advocated the establishment of an independent, democratic republic founded on egalitarian principles in the United States: "We have it in our power to begin the world over again." It sold 120,000 copies in the Thirteen Colonies in three months, and may have been read by half the population. The point, of course, is that they *could* read.

Common Sense

What was really happening, as literacy rates rose and printed books became widely available, was that the ability to hold a discussion among equals about ends and means, the fundamental basis for decision-making in hunter-gatherer societies, was being restored to their distant descendants in Western mass societies. It was still impossible for millions of people to gather in the same place and hold a sensible debate, but books could present and discuss ideas for their consideration, and those ideas could come to animate entire mass societies. A new, far more diffuse version of Boehm's "reverse dominance hierarchy" could make egalitarian values compatible even with mass societies.

And that's what happened. Once mass societies cracked the problem of numbers and regained the ability to discuss their affairs and make decisions collectively, the pyramidal structure of power and privilege in civilized states—never popular with most people—was no longer an unavoidable necessity. Societies could become self-directing—democratic, in other words—and as soon as that became possible, people remembered that they had always preferred equality to hierarchy. The revolutions began, and although many were crushed, they kept coming. Today a significant portion of the world's population lives in societies that are more or less democratic, and almost all the others pretend to be.

The revival of the principle of equality did not automatically make its beneficiaries peaceful, as the example of revolutionary France clearly demonstrates—but then, our hunter-gatherer ancestors were not exactly peaceful either. It opened up some interesting new possibilities if democracy ever became the dominant political form on the planet, but that lay far in the future. At the time, unfortunately, the main effect of popular revolution was to show European states how to exploit pseudo-egalitarianism, better known as nationalism, and get whole populations involved in waging war.

Nationalism Ascendant

Once Napoleon had declared himself Emperor of the French, it became safer for the countries he attacked to arm their own people. The revolution was over, and the French armies were no longer liberators, just foreigners attacking the motherland. The surviving kings had climbed the learning curve and now understood that they could exploit the nascent national feelings of their own people to mobilize resistance against the French. In Spain, for example, which was occupied by French troops for half a decade, civilian resistance fighters began waging a nationalist *guerrilla* ("little war") in the name of the exiled king. Backed by Wellington's British army based in Portugal, they killed as many French soldiers over the years as died in Napoleon's catastrophic Russian campaign.

When Napoleon, having temporarily subdued every other country on the continent, finally invaded Russia in 1812 with 440,000 men, Russian nationalism was mobilized to similar effect. The campaign is known in Russian history as the "Great Patriotic War," and the fighting was made more pitiless by a national antagonism that had simply not existed back in the time of limited wars and professional armies. The battle of Borodino, the Russians' last stand before Moscow fell, is described in the two eyewitness accounts below. They lost thirty-five thousand men, and the French, thirty thousand.

> When we reached the crest of the ravine, we were riddled with grapeshot from the battery [in front of us] and several others flanking it, but nothing stopped us. Despite my wounded leg I did as well as my [men] in jumping out of the way of

roundshot which ricocheted into our ranks. Whole files, half platoons even, went down under the enemy's fire, and left huge gaps ... A Russian line tried to stop us, but at thirty yards' range we fired a volley and passed through. Then we dashed towards the redoubt and clambered through the embrasures. I went in just after a piece had been discharged. The Russian gunners received us with handspikes and rammers, and we fought them hand to hand. They were redoubtable opponents. A great many Frenchmen fell into rifle pits, jumbled up with the Russians already occupying them.

Capt. Charles François, 30th Regiment[8]

It was horrible to see that enormous mass of riddled soldiers. French and Russians were cast together, and there were many wounded men who were incapable of moving and lay in that wild chaos intermingled with the bodies of horses and the wreckage of shattered cannon.

Field Marshal Prince Michael Barclay de Tolly, Russian Minister of War and Commander-in-Chief, 1810–15[9]

Napoleon won all the battles, including Borodino, and even occupied Moscow, but the Russians would not accept that they were beaten. On the orders of de Tolly, they destroyed their own crops and food stocks rather than leave them to the French, and Napoleon was eventually forced to retreat in the dead of winter through lack of supplies. Only a few thousand of the French made it out of Russia alive.

Enter the Prussians

By calling up the class of 1814 a year early and canceling all exemptions from the draft, Napoleon managed to come up with one last large army in the spring of 1813, but even France was now

The retreat of Napoleon's Grande Armée from Russia in 1812, by Johann Klein

running out of manpower. Some of the new recruits got as little as one week's training before being thrown into battle. Even more seriously, the Prussians finally brought in conscription. There was no kingdom in Europe more autocratic, more riddled with class privileges and inequalities, than Prussia, but the law of 1813 made all male Prussians liable for three years' service in the regular army upon reaching twenty, followed by two years in the active reserve and fourteen years in the *Landwehr* (territorial army).[10]

At the opening of the new war against Napoleon, the Prussian army reformers created a new decoration for bravery that broke all the rules of Prussian society by being open equally to peasants, bourgeoisie, and nobles: the Order of the Iron Cross. Their decree stated:

> In the present great catastrophe in which everything is at stake for the Nation, the vigorous spirit which elevates the Nation so high deserves to be honored and perpetuated by some quite peculiar monuments. That the perseverance by

> which the Nation endured the irresistible evils of an iron age did not shrink to timidity is proved by the high courage which now animates every breast and which could survive only because it was based on religion and true loyalty to King and Country.[11]

Certificate of Iron Cross 2nd class for Edgar Wintrath, October 1918

The reformers were gambling that a combination of patriotism and compulsion would make conscription work even without the revolutionary ideal of the equality of all citizens, that men would be seduced by the promise of an equality in battle that they were denied in their ordinary lives. They turned out to be right.

"Get me a national army," Marshal Blücher had begged the Prussian reformers, and in 1813 he had one: the *Landwehr* battalions of conscripts tripled the size of his army and played a major part in the two decisive defeats of Napoleon in the Battle of the Nations at Leipzig in 1813 and at Waterloo in 1815.

> The *Landwehr* battalions were so-so at first, but after they had tasted plenty of powder, they did as well as the battalions of the Line.
>
> Marshal Blücher[12]

The battles of the Revolutionary and Napoleonic wars were larger on average than those of the eighteenth century, but they were fundamentally the same sort of battle and the weapons were virtually identical. The great change was in the *number* of battles. In classical times or in the Thirty Years' War, there might be three or four battles in a year, and encounters where the opposing armies exceeded one hundred thousand men in total were rare. During the period of 1792–1814 there were forty-nine such battles, and smaller but still major battles occurred on average more than once a week on one or another of the several fronts where campaigns were in progress.[13] At least four million people were killed, and the great majority of them were soldiers—a figure quite unprecedented in history. Yet European society did not break down under the strain. The European states had developed the wealth, the organizational techniques, and the methods of motivation needed to fight mass wars with a degree of popular participation that no other civilized society had ever achieved.

MASS LITERACY & PRINTING

reignites long-dormant egalitarian ideals

democratic revolutionary regimes with huge armies

autocratic regimes stir up popular patriotism to help them compete

bigger armies all around, with men motivated by passionate national allegiance

MORE BATTLES. MORE DEATHS.

> He who uses force unsparingly, without reference against the bloodshed involved, must obtain a superiority if his adversary uses less vigour in its application ... To introduce into a philosophy of war a principle of moderation would be an absurdity. War is an act of violence pushed to its utmost bounds.
>
> Karl von Clausewitz, 1819[14]

Karl von Clausewitz was a Prussian veteran of the Napoleonic wars whose writings on the theory of war became gospel for succeeding generations of soldiers. But one form of restriction on the scale of violence did survive for most of the nineteenth century: by and large, civilians were spared the worst horrors of war.

There were three reasons for this. First, the industrial production of weapons and equipment was still much less important than the role of the masses of soldiers themselves. Second, the armies lacked weapons that could reach the enemy's centers of production in any case. And finally, the soldiers were genuinely reluctant to turn their weapons against civilians. Unfortunately, when the first two conditions changed, the last proved to be no obstacle.

For forty years after the defeat of Napoleon's comeback attempt at Waterloo in 1815, there was peace between the major European states. There was a huge conservative reaction against the excesses of the French Revolution, and among the dangerous innovations generally discarded was the mass army based on conscription; most of Europe went back to small, professional armies. But by the time the spate of mid-century wars arrived in 1854–70, every major power in Europe except Britain, protected by its navy, had reintroduced conscription—and by this time new technology was beginning to filter into war.

American Civil War

The greatest of the mid-century wars was not fought in Europe at all. It was the American Civil War, in which 622,000 American soldiers died—more than in both world wars, Korea, Vietnam, Afghanistan, and Iraq—out of a population only one tenth as big as it is now. Both sides soon resorted to conscription, and the resulting armies were huge. The US Army enlisted almost two million men during the four years of the war, and the Confederates, almost a million, out of a total population of only thirty-one million. And one fifth of those who enlisted died.

During the previous decade, new rifled muskets had come into general use, effectively quintupling the range at which the average infantryman could hit his opponent, and within months, defending infantry were taking shelter behind natural obstacles whenever possible. In practice, the range at which infantry opened fire didn't change much from the days of smoothbore muskets: the average opening range of engagement was only 127 yards. But accuracy had improved greatly, and most soldiers were taking aimed shots. A great many of them hit their targets.[15]

The infantry's new habit of taking cover whenever possible set the course of battles like Second Manassas in August 1862, when Stonewall Jackson's Virginians lined up behind the shelter of a railway cutting to receive the attack of three times as many Northern infantry. At the height of the attack, some Northern officer rode forward through the black powder smoke, well ahead of his troops, and reached the lip of the railway cutting miraculously untouched. For a few seconds he paused there, sword in hand, as useless as he was brave. Some of the Southern soldiers just below him began to yell out, "Don't kill him! Don't kill him!"[16] But within seconds both he and his horse were shot down by less romantic men.

> I had taken part in two great battles, and heard the bullets whistle both days, and yet I had scarcely seen a Rebel save killed, wounded or prisoners. I remember even line officers, who were at the battle of Chancellorsville, said: "Why, we never saw any Rebels where we were; only smoke and bushes, and lots of our men tumbling about," and now I appreciate this most fully . . . Put a man in a hole, and a good battery on a hill behind him, and he will beat off three times his number even if he is not a very good soldier.
>
> Col. Theodore Lyman, 1869[17]

Along with the muzzle-loading single-shot rifles that produced such havoc at Second Manassas, the forerunners of practically every modern weapon were used in the American Civil War. There were breech-loading, magazine-fed rifles like the seven-shot Henry repeater, early hand-cranked machine guns like the Gatling gun, rifled breech-loading cannons, submarines, ironclad warships, and even a primitive form of aerial reconnaissance using hot-air balloons. The extensive American railway network allowed troops to be moved quickly over long distances—Civil War battles were the first in history in which the infantry did not get there entirely on foot—and the telegraph let generals coordinate the movements of large forces spread out over a wide area.

In a sense, the Civil War happened just in time. Had it been delayed another ten or fifteen years, most of those new weapons would have been available in large numbers and reliable models, and it would have looked like World War I. As it was, they were mostly rare or unreliable. The artillery was particularly ineffective, having not a much greater range than the infantry's rifled muskets. Out of 144,000 American soldiers whose cause of death is known, 108,000 were killed by rifle bullets, and only 12,500 by shell fragments and 7,000 by swords and bayonets.

Twenty years later, when field artillery could fire accurately for over a mile and shell bursts could produce a thousand fragments lethal at a radius of twenty feet, the figures would have been very different. Even without modem artillery, Civil War battlefields took on an ominously modern aspect by the end: in the lines around Petersburg in 1865, the field entrenchments grew so elaborate—complete with dugouts, wire entanglements, and listening posts—that they foreshadowed the trenches of World War I.

Soldiers in the trenches before battle at Petersburg, Virginia, 1865

The Civil War also demonstrated how hard it would be in the future to gain a decisive victory even against a relatively weak opponent. The North effectively outnumbered the South four-to-one in military manpower (since the Confederacy did not draw on its large black slave population for soldiers) and at least six-to-one in industrial resources. In the year before the Southern states seceded, the North produced 94 percent of the united country's steel, 97 percent of its coal, and 97 percent of its firearms.[18] Yet it took four years of high-intensity war to bring the South to its knees.

It also took ruthless economic warfare. From the start, the North clamped a tight blockade on the South to strangle its overseas trade. By the end General William Tecumseh Sherman (whom the Confederate president, Jefferson Davis, called the "Attila [the Hun] of the American Continent") was deliberately devastating huge areas of the deep South. "We are not only fighting hostile armies but a hostile people," said Sherman, "and must make old and young, rich and poor, feel the hard hand of war."[19]

To those who protested that his "scorched earth" methods were immoral, Sherman simply replied: "If the people raise a howl against my barbarity and cruelty, I will answer that war is war ... If they want peace, they and their relatives must stop the war."[20] He was born before his time.

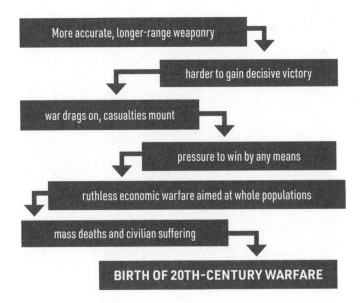

More accurate, longer-range weaponry

harder to gain decisive victory

war drags on, casualties mount

pressure to win by any means

ruthless economic warfare aimed at whole populations

mass deaths and civilian suffering

BIRTH OF 20TH-CENTURY WARFARE

CHAPTER 7

Total War

The Continuous Front

> At first there will be increased slaughter—increased slaughter on so terrible a scale as to render it impossible to get troops to push the battle to a decisive issue. They will try to, thinking that they are fighting under the old conditions, and they will learn such a lesson that they will abandon the attempt forever. Then . . . we shall have . . . a long period of continually increasing strain upon the resources of the combatants . . . Everybody will be entrenched in the next war.
>
> I. S. Bloch, 1897[1]

These predictions about the next great war, published in Russian in 1897 by Ivan Bloch, a Warsaw banker and ardent pacifist, were logically unassailable. The great powers would call up millions of soldiers and rush them to the frontiers by rail when war came. Given the firepower now available to each man, eventual stalemate was inevitable: the defensive was far stronger than the offensive. But professional soldiers didn't take Bloch's work seriously, and every army attacked simultaneously in 1914, convinced that a quick series of decisive battles would settle the war within six months.

The First World War was not about trade or overseas colonies or stopping some would-be conqueror. Nobody wanted or was planning for a war in 1914. Wars between two neighboring countries often have specific, more or less rational causes; multiplayer alliance systems, from Yanomamo villages to twentieth-century European great powers, can stumble into system-wide wars quite unintentionally.

France feared Germany because its population and industry were growing faster, so it made an alliance with Russia, on the far side of Germany. Germany felt encircled and made an alliance with Austria-Hungary, which wanted German backing because it was competing with Russia for bits of territory in the Balkans. And Britain made an "entente" (almost an alliance) with France and Russia because it also felt threatened by the rise of Germany. This was all just prudent contingency planning, not rabid aggression—but if anybody got into a fight, even with some country outside the alliance system (as Austria-Hungary did with Serbia in 1914), it might easily pull all the members of both alliances into a great war.

It did exactly that, in just over one month, because the whole system was on a hair trigger. It should not have been, but the prevailing (although mistaken) belief was that decisive, war-ending battles would happen fast, so the first countries to mobilize and attack would have a huge advantage. In fact the principal artifacts that ended the war of movement and drove the soldier of the First World War down into the trenches—bolt-action repeating rifles, air- and water-cooled machine guns, quick-firing and long-range artillery, barbed wire, and the like—were already present in embryo on American Civil War battlefields and in fully mature versions by the Russo-Japanese War of 1904–5, but both of those precedents were largely ignored because they took place outside of Europe. Despite Bloch's warning, few soldiers had any idea what they were getting into when they went off to war in 1914.

We listen for an eternity to the iron sledgehammers beating on our trench. Percussion and time fuses, 105's, 150's, 210's— all the calibres. Amid this tempest of ruin we instantly recognize the shell that is coming to bury us. As soon as we pick out its dismal howl, we look at each other in agony. All curled and shrivelled up we crouch under the very weight of its breath, helmets clang together; we stagger about like drunks. The beams tremble, a cloud of choking smoke fills the dugout, the candles go out.

French veteran[2]

The German army grew sixfold in the first two weeks of August 1914 as reservists joined their regiments. By mid-August trains had delivered 1,485,000 German soldiers to the borders with France and Belgium. The French, Austrians, and Russians performed similar miracles of organization—but by October the armies had all ground to a halt.

Machine weapons—quick-firing artillery and machine-guns firing six hundred bullets a minute—filled the air with a lethal steel sleet. Anybody trying to move aboveground was almost certain to be hit. Killing had been mechanized and men became the prisoners of machines, trapped below ground level in the proliferating trenches.

By early 1915 the military authorities were starting to understand that they faced a completely new strategic problem: the continuous front. There were no enemy flanks that you could get around, just two trench systems stretching 475 miles from the English Channel to the border of neutral Switzerland. The front lines were usually a few hundred yards apart, but in some places less than a hundred.

The continuous front was the result of simple mathematics. Firepower grew by leaps and bounds in the latter half of the nineteenth century, enabling infantrymen to control much more frontage. They didn't need to be shoulder to shoulder anymore: by the time of the South African War in 1899, with rifles that could deliver ten shots a minute at a thousand yards, the Boers were finding that they could stop British frontal attacks with only one rifleman every three yards.[3]

Multiply the width of the front that an individual infantryman could now hold by the millions of men who would be available in a European war, and the continuous front was inevitable. Armies could now spread out to fill all the space available, and so they did—not only in France, but across the vast distances of Russia, and later across northern Italy, northern Greece, northeastern Turkey, Mesopotamia (Iraq), and Palestine.

For the men in the trenches, it was a new kind of war. Apart from during sieges, armies had previously been in contact with the enemy for only a few days each year. Now the soldiers were in the trenches, within shouting distance of the enemy, all the time. Each day they faced the risk of being killed, and each day they endured the misery of living in a ditch.

> Constantly having your feet in this gruel-like muck caused a complaint which became known as "trench foot." There were dozens of amputation cases in the regiment.
>
> British veteran

> Rats bother you; rats eat you if you get wounded and nobody can look after you. It was a dirty lousy place to live, with all the corruption that is known to mankind.
>
> British veteran

A War of Artillery

The continuous front meant that no movement was possible until you had broken through the enemy lines facing you—and *every* attack had to be a frontal attack. The generals quickly found out that their infantry would be slaughtered if they tried to advance unaided; the only way to break through was to eliminate the enemy's firepower by smashing the enemy's trenches and gun positions with shellfire before the attack. So the trench war became a war of artillery.

Over half the casualties were now caused by shellfire, and shell production could not keep up with demand. Prewar French planning had assumed the army would use around ten thousand 75-mm. shells a day; by 1915 France was producing two hundred thousand a day and still not keeping up with demand. The nineteen-day British bombardment that began the third Battle of Ypres in 1917 used 4.3 million shells weighing 107,000 tons, a year's production for fifty-five thousand workers.[4]

Still they couldn't get a real breakthrough. The bombardment would destroy most of the enemy's machine guns in the first-line trenches, but enough defenders always survived to make the advance a slow and costly business. Even if the attacking infantry managed to capture the enemy's first-line trenches in just one day, that gave the enemy's reserves enough time to man a whole new trench system just to the rear. For more than three years, no offensive shifted the Western Front by as much as ten miles.

> . . . the ruddy clouds of brick-dust hang over the shelled villages by day and at night the eastern horizon roars and bubbles with light. And everywhere in these desolate places I see the faces and figures of enslaved men, the marching columns pearl-hued with chalky dust on the sweat of their heavy drab clothes; the files of carrying parties laden and

staggering in the flickering moonlight of gunfire; the "waves" of assaulting troops lying silent and pale on the tapelines of the jumping-off places.

I crouch with them while the steel glacier rushing by just overhead scrapes away every syllable, every fragment of a message bawled in my ear ... I go forward with them ... up and down across ground like a huge ruined honeycomb, and my wave melts away, and the second wave comes up, and also melts away, and then the third wave merges into the ruins of the first and second, and after a while the fourth blunders into the remnants of the others, and we begin to run forward to catch up with the barrage, gasping and sweating, in bunches, anyhow, every bit of the months of drill and rehearsal forgotten.

We come to wire that is uncut, and beyond we see grey coal-scuttle helmets bobbing about ... and the loud crackling of machine guns changes as to a screeching of steam being blown off by a hundred engines and soon no one is left standing. An hour later our guns are "back on the first objective," and the brigade, with all its hopes and beliefs, has found its grave on northern slopes of the Somme battlefield.[5]

Henry Williamson, *The Wet Flanders Plain*

New weapons like poison gas only increased the casualties without breaking the deadlock, and the war became a simple matter of attrition. In the battle of the Somme in 1916, the British captured forty-five square miles in a five-month battle at a cost of 415,000 men—over 8,000 men for each useless square mile—but the Germans were compelled to sacrifice men and equipment at a similar rate. Since Britain, France, and Russia had twice the population of Germany and its allies, the likelihood was that sufficient battles on that scale should eventually give them the upper hand (although nobody ever said this out loud).

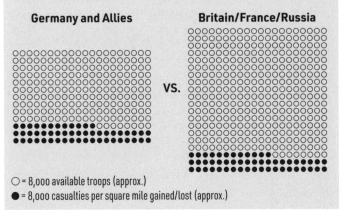

THE BRUTAL MATHEMATICS OF ATTRITION

Germany and Allies   **Britain/France/Russia**

VS.

○ = 8,000 available troops (approx.)
● = 8,000 casualties per square mile gained/lost (approx.)

Civilians

The war of attrition involved not only soldiers but civilians. As fit young men vanished into the armies—France put 20 percent of its entire population into uniform and Germany 18 percent—the civilian economy was effectively conscripted too. Labor and raw materials were allocated not by the market but by government orders, and rationing was imposed on food and scarce consumer goods. Millions of women became factory workers

. Female munitions workers operating lathes in a British shell factory

for the first time to replace the men who had gone off to war. People began to use the new phrase "home front" because the role of munitions workers, and of manufacturing more generally, was as important to victory as the soldiers in the trenches. But all "fronts" can be attacked—and they duly were.

The economic war was fought mostly at sea: both sides immediately imposed blockades on the other's seaborne trade. The British stopped all ships bound for German ports, and in the last two years of the war undernourishment caused an excess of eight hundred thousand civilian deaths in Germany over the peacetime mortality rate.[6] The Germans, with a smaller navy, resorted to submarines to cut Britain off from its overseas suppliers of food and raw materials. The U-boats sank fifteen million tons of shipping during the war but they never managed to staunch the flow of supplies, and Germany's policy of "unrestricted" submarine warfare, announced in January 1917, brought the United States into the war against it. That more than made up for the Allied loss of Russian troops when the Bolshevik revolution took Russia out of the war later that year—and the losses of ships bound for Britain plummeted after the Royal Navy revived the time-honored convoy system in September 1917.

There was, however, now another way of attacking the enemy's economy: go after the factories and the war workers directly. Only twelve years after the Wright Brothers made the first powered flight, Germany already possessed aircraft able to fly hundreds of miles and drop bombs on enemy cities: the zeppelins. Inevitably, it used them.

> The idea was to equip from twelve to twenty Zeppelins and drill their crews to function as a co-ordinated task force. Each ship would carry about 300 fire bombs. They would attack simultaneously at night. Hence, as many as six thousand

IT IS FAR BETTER
TO FACE THE BULLETS
THAN TO BE KILLED
AT HOME BY A BOMB

JOIN THE ARMY AT ONCE
& HELP TO STOP AN AIR RAID

GOD SAVE THE KING

The first major air raid on London came in September 1915, when Zeppelin L15 dropped fifteen high-explosive bombs and fifty-odd incendiaries on London at night and caused seventeen casualties. Later raids involved more zeppelins and two- and three-engined bombers, but only four thousand British civilians were killed or injured in the whole war. Nevertheless, the raids were the precedent for

Top: Zeppelins are unlikely poster boys for the British recruitment drive, 1915.
Bottom: The wreck of a Zeppelin L33 in Essex, one of two brought down on the night of September 23–24, 1916.

Rotterdam, for Dresden, for Hiroshima, for all the cities that were destroyed from the air in the twentieth century—and for the strategy of nuclear deterrence too. After 1915, everybody was a legitimate target.

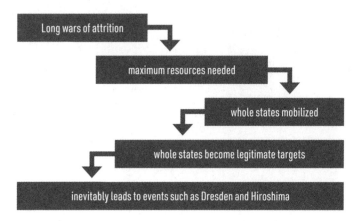

Long wars of attrition

maximum resources needed

whole states mobilized

whole states become legitimate targets

inevitably leads to events such as Dresden and Hiroshima

Landships

> Panic spread like an electric current, passing from man to man along the trench. As the churning tracks reared overhead the bravest men clambered above ground to launch suicidal counter-attacks, hurling grenades onto the tanks' roofs or shooting and stabbing at any vision slit within reach. They were shot down or crushed, while others threw up their hands in terrified surrender or bolted down the communication trenches towards the second line.
>
> German infantryman's first encounter with a tank, 1916[8]

The solution to the problem posed by the trenches occurred to a British staff officer, Col. E. D. Swinton, only a month or two after the trenches appeared in late 1914. What was needed, obviously, was a vehicle armored against machine-gun bullets and carrying its own guns, which could roll over shell holes, barbed wire, and trenches on caterpillar tracks. The earliest production models of the "landships," as they were first called, reached the Western Front in late 1916, but they didn't go into battle in really large numbers until the battle of Cambrai in November 1917, where 476 were committed.

The first official photograph taken of a tank going into action, at the Battle of Flers-Courcelette on September 15, 1916. The tank is a Mark I.

At Cambrai, also for the first time, there was a complete fireplan for artillery to engage the German defenses simultaneously all the way back to the furthest reserve positions, and the 150 batteries of guns that reinforced the sector arrived secretly. In order to achieve complete surprise, these extra guns did not open fire in the usual way to "register" their targets (that is, fire a few rounds and see if the shells are landing in the right places). Instead, they depended entirely on aerial reconnaissance, accurate mapping, and ballistic calculations, and all one thousand guns opened fire at the same time on the morning of the attacks. It was the first large-scale use of "predicted fire," and with the help of the tanks and 289 aircraft used as artillery spotters, ground-attack aircraft and bombers, the attack almost broke through the German lines completely. Only a very rapid and ferocious German counterattack closed the breach.

The tanks and predicted fire at Cambrai enabled the British army to advance six miles in six hours, at a cost of four thousand dead and wounded. Earlier the same year, at the Third Battle of Ypres, the British had taken three months to advance a similar distance, and they lost a quarter of a million men doing it. After that the trench stalemate was over, for the Germans had just solved the breakthrough problem in the same way, though with less reliance on tanks. Beginning with an offensive at Riga on the Russian front in September 1917, a Germany artillery officer named Col. Georg Bruchmueller had independently devised a similar formula for surprise and rapid penetration: massive amounts of indirect and predicted artillery fire with no warning beforehand, and infantry "storm troops" who bypassed enemy strongpoints and just kept moving ever deeper into the defended zone, spreading confusion and dismay, and ultimately driving the enemy into a major retreat.

German tanks never matched the British in numbers or quality, but it was Germany that took the offensive in the spring of 1918 (after three years on the defensive), in an all-out gamble to win the war before large numbers of American troops arrived in France. At Arras in March 1918, 6,608 German guns fired 3.2 million rounds on the first day of the offensive—and the Germans gained more ground in two weeks than the Allies had taken in all their offensives during the whole war. Further fast-moving offensives followed and the Allies nearly lost the war in the spring of 1918, but the Germans failed to reach either Paris or the Channel coast—and they suffered a million casualties between March and July of 1918.[9]

After that, the Allies went on the offensive, mainly using British, Canadian, and Australian troops to spearhead the

German boy soldiers in WWI

attacks, and showed the same ability to gain ground. The plans for 1919, had the war continued, called for a force of several thousand tanks closely supported by aircraft to smash through the enemy's front, with infantry following closely in armored personnel carriers, but that was not necessary. By November 1918 the German army was collapsing, the navy had mutinied, and Berlin asked for an armistice.

Tremendous Victory, Bad Peace?

Why was the peace treaty that followed so extreme, with "war guilt" clauses and huge reparations and entire empires dismantled? Why did the peace last only twenty years?

The national rivalries, military fears, and territorial disputes that had caused World War I were not more important than those that caused the Seven Years' War a century and a half before. In that earlier style of war, though, small professional armies had fought each other offstage while civilians everywhere largely ignored it. Eventually the losers would hand over a few bits of territory to the winners and peace would return. A hundred thousand soldiers would be dead but the people who mattered didn't care about them much, and no regime fell.

The conflict of 1914–18, on the other hand, was the first total war, and the governments of Europe discovered to their dismay that it was almost impossible to stop short of total victory for one side and total surrender for the other. When sixty million men have been conscripted into the armies and almost half of them have been either killed (eight million) or wounded (twenty million), and when people's willingness to bear these huge losses has been kept up in every country by hate propaganda that paints the war as a moral crusade against absolute evil—then governments cannot just sort out the petty Balkan quarrel that triggered it, swap around a few colonies, and send the surviving soldiers home.

Total war meant victory also had to be total: the survival of not just the government but the entire regime depended on it. Even when governments could see military collapse or social revolution looming, they refused to consider a compromise peace. The collapses and revolutions duly came.

Collapse and Revolution

The Russian army was the first to collapse, in early 1917, and near-starvation at home brought the (first) Russian revolution in March 1917. In April, half the divisions of the French army mutinied after another forlorn offensive, and nearly twenty-five thousand men faced court-martials after order was restored. In May, four hundred thousand Italian troops simply fled the battlefield at Caporetto. Even in Britain, political stability was no longer a certainty: later that month the Chief of the Imperial General Staff in London wrote to Gen. Sir Douglas Haig, the commander of the British army in France: "I am afraid there is no getting away from the fact that there is some unrest in the country now as a result partly of the Russian revolution."[10]

All the empires on the losing side—German, Russian, Austrian, and Ottoman—were destroyed by the war, and the latter three were chopped up into more than a dozen new countries and territories. About half the people of Europe, the Middle East, and Africa found themselves living under a radically different regime or even as the citizens of a different country. The totalitarian controls that had been imposed during the war continued in peacetime in the new Soviet Union, and were brought back later by fascist regimes in Italy and Germany. And the losers were so unhappy about the peace settlement that the fighting resumed after only two decades.

Blitzkrieg

Confronted with an unprecedented military problem, the soldiers of the First World War had solved the trench stalemate, and the professionals in every country debated how best to exploit tanks to restore mobility to warfare. In the early years of the Second World War (1939–41) it seemed as if the Germans, at least, had come up with the right answer.

"*Blitzkrieg*" (lightning war) operated by using a highly mobile force of tanks, infantry, and artillery, all on tracks or wheels, to break through the enemy's defenses on a narrow front. Ground-attack aircraft (Stukas) gave close support, and the essence of the operation was speed. Don't get held up by enemy strongpoints; just go around them and keep moving. You should be through the heavily defended zone in hours, and then the armored column pushes on at high speed, spreading chaos behind the enemy's front and overrunning its higher command posts and communications far behind the front. In theory, and usually in practice in the early days of Blitzkrieg, the enemy front will then collapse when the troops holding it realize that they have been cut off from their own headquarters and supplies.

The German Blitzkrieg destroyed the entire Polish army in three weeks in 1939 at a cost of only eight thousand German dead. The following spring in France it was even more success-ful: the French and British had more and better tanks, but the Germans' superior tactics enabled them to conquer the Low Countries and France in only six weeks. Long wars of attrition seemed to be a thing of the past, but it wasn't so simple. The tanks were setting the continuous front in motion, and civilians, not troops in trenches, were its main victims.

The Return of Attrition

By the middle of the war, when German forces were fighting deep inside the Soviet Union, attrition was back. The Russians had learned to deal with Blitzkrieg by making the defended zone many miles deep, with successive belts of trenches, minefields, bunkers, gun positions, and tank traps that would slow down the armored spearheads and eventually wear them away. Tanks had evened the odds again, in the sense that they restored the power of the offensive and made breakthroughs possible, but they did not abolish the continuous front. Sometimes there would be a successful breakthrough, but even if there was, the whole enemy front would generally retreat some dozens or hundreds of miles and then stabilize again.

The armies of the Western allies got off lightly, because they had no—or relatively few—troops fighting on the ground in continental Europe (much of which was occupied by the Germans) between May 1940 and June 1944, but on the Eastern Front the losses were enormous. The Russians, for example, built around 100,000 tanks, 100,000 aircraft, and 175,000 artillery pieces during the war, of which at least two-thirds were destroyed in the fighting, but fully mobilized industrial societies could absorb enormous punishment and still keep going. The Germans ended up with two thirds of all men between the ages of eighteen and forty-five in the armed forces and lost three and a half million military dead,[11] but their army was still fighting in April 1945 when the two fronts facing the Soviet advance from the east and the Anglo American advance from the west were practically back-to-back down the middle of a devastated Germany.

Civilians and the Continuous Front

ASS, TUESDAY, JULY 8, 1943   14 PAGES   THREE CENTS   Today

GERMANY'S LONG-DELAYED OFFENSIVE AGAINST RUSSIA OPENS ON 165-MILE FRONT

U.S.-Japanese Sea Battle   586 NAZI TANKS

Springfield Union headline at the start of Operation Barbarossa

And high though the military casualties were, civilian losses were even worse. As continuous fronts ground across whole countries, they destroyed almost everything in their path.

> Guts splattered across the rubble and sprayed from one dying man onto another; tightly riveted machines ripped like the belly of a cow which has just been sliced open, flaming and groaning; trees broken into tiny fragments; gaping windows pouring out torrents of billowing dust, dispersing into oblivion all that remains of a comfortable parlour . . . the cries of officers and non-coms, trying to shout across the cataclysm to regroup their sections and companies. That is how we took part in the German advance, being called through the noise and dust, following the clouds churned up by our tanks to the northern outskirts of Belgorod . . .

> The burnt-out ruins of Belgorod fell into the hands of [our surviving troops] on the second evening... We had been ordered to reduce the pockets of resistance in the ashes of a suburb called Deptreotka, if I remember correctly. When we reached the end of our sweep, we collapsed at the bottom of a large crater and stared at each other for a long time in dazed silence. None of us could speak . . . The air still roared and shook and smelled of burning... By the fourth or fifth evening, we had gone through Belgorod without even knowing it.
>
> Guy Sajer, an Alsatian conscript in the German army[12]

German troops had first reached Belgorod, a city of thirty-four thousand people in southern Russia, in October 1941, three months after the invasion began, but on that ocassion the city was lucky. There were two days of fighting, but most of the buildings and most of the citizens survived. Soviet troops liberated it in March 1943 as the front moved back west after the German Sixth Army was destroyed at Stalingrad. Once again Belgorod got away virtually unharmed: the Germans were retreating so fast that they didn't have time to destroy it.

Sajer's description above relates to the third invasion, in July 1943, when Belgorod was retaken by the *Gross Deutschland* Division in the Battle of Kursk, the last great German offensive of the war. Six thousand tanks, thirty thousand guns, and two million men fought along a front of hundreds of miles. The German armored spearheads were finally halted by the deep Russian defenses, and the Soviet counterattack liberated Belgorod again in mid-August. This time the Germans attempted to hold it, and street-fighting killed three thousand soldiers within the city limits. By the time the battle was over, only 140 of Belgorod's thirty-four thousand people were left alive in the ruins. The rest were refugees, conscripts, or dead.

Belgorod had no military importance, but the front moved across it four times and practically obliterated it. The same thing happened to thousands of other towns and villages in Europe: World War II killed at least twice as many soldiers as World War I, but it also killed almost twice as many civilians as soldiers. Six million of those civilians were Jews deliberately murdered by the Nazis on "racial" grounds, in what has become known as the Holocaust. These deaths, and those of another four million Poles, Russians, Roma, gay men, and disabled people deemed undesirable by the Nazis, were not technically part of the war, but it was the wartime circumstances that provided cover for the whole operation, just as the First World War provided cover for the Armenian genocide.

On average the countries from Germany eastward, where the fighting was most intense and prolonged, lost about 10 percent of their populations in the Second World War. Wars involving big regular armies in continuous fronts have been quite scarce since 1945, but on the few occasions when they fought in continuous fronts in densely populated countries (the Korean War, for example), civilian casualties have been just as high.

Strategic Bombardment

The disintegration of nations in the last war was brought about by the actions of the armies in the field. [In the future] it will be accomplished directly by . . . aerial forces . . . War will be waged essentially against the unarmed populations of the cities and great industrial centers . . . A complete breakdown of the social order cannot but take place in a country subjected to this kind of merciless pounding . . . It will be an inhuman, atrocious performance, but these are the facts.

Gen. Giulio Douhet. 1921[13]

At least 97 percent of the seventy million people who were killed in World War II were *not* killed by air raids on cities, and bombing did not win the war against Germany. But that was only because the technology was not up to it yet; the will to do it was certainly there.

"Strategic bombardment"—destroying the enemy's homeland—is the natural weapon of total war. Its most influential advocate was an Italian general called Giulio Douhet, who had proposed an independent Italian bombing force of five hundred multi-engine aircraft as early as 1915. His greatest influence, however, was in Britain and the United States, technologically oriented countries that would rather spend money than lives in war. The principal American bomber of World War II, the B-17, was flight-tested in 1935, and the Royal Air Force's four-engined bombers were designed in the same year.

The German blitz on British cities between September 1940 and May 1941 killed forty thousand civilians, but that was only one in a thousand of the population. (The British had expected fourteen times as many casualties, and had made plans for mass graves.) The short-range, twin-engine German bombers had been designed for battlefield use, and were simply not up to the job.

British bombers were bigger and longer-range, but strong German air defenses forced them to bomb at night so they rarely hit their designated targets (factories, railway stations, etc.). In early 1942, Air Marshal Sir Arthur Harris took over Bomber Command, and dropped the pretense that the bombing had any more precise objective than the German civilian population. The new policy conformed entirely with the ideas first expressed by Douhet.

The "mass bombing" strategy that Harris launched with the thousand-bomber raid on Cologne in April 1942 killed 593,000 German civilians and destroyed 3.3 million homes in the following three years, but it wasn't really cost-effective. Up to one third of British manpower and industrial resources was devoted to supporting Bomber Command in the latter years of the war, and fifty-five thousand British and Canadian aircrew were killed. In the worst period (March 1943–February 1944) only 16 percent of crews survived a thirty-mission tour.[14] And only very rarely did their efforts have the full effect Harris intended.

In the north German city of Hamburg, on a clear, dry summer night on July 28, 1943, the unusually tight concentration of British bombs in a densely populated working-class district created something new: a firestorm. It covered four square miles, with an air temperature at the center of 1,475°F and convection winds blowing inward with hurricane force. One survivor compared the noise of the firestorm to "an old organ in a church when someone is playing all the notes at once." Nobody who stayed in the underground shelters survived; they were cremated or died of carbon monoxide poisoning. Those who went up into the streets, on the other hand, could be swept by the wind into the heart of the firestorm.

> Mother wrapped me in wet sheets, kissed me, and said, "Run!" I hesitated at the door: In front of me I could see only fire— everything red, like the door to a furnace. An intense heat struck me. A burning beam fell in front of my feet. I shied back but then, when I was ready to jump over it, it was whirled away by a ghostly hand. The sheets around me acted as sails and I had the feeling that I was being carried away by the storm. I reached the front of a five-storey building . . . which . . . had been bombed and burned out in a previous raid and there was not much in it for the fire to get hold of. Someone came out, grabbed me in their arms, and pulled me into the doorway.
>
> Traute Koch, fifteen in 1943[15]

Ruined residential and commercial buildings in Hamburg after British Operation Gomorrah, 1943

Twenty thousand people died in Hamburg in two hours. If the RAF could have done that every time, the war would have ended in six months, but on only one more occasion, at Dresden in 1945, were all the conditions right for a firestorm. The usual consequences were far less impressive. On average, a single British bomber sortie with a seven-man crew killed three Germans, maybe one of whom was a factory worker—and after an average of fourteen missions, the bomber crew themselves would be dead or, if they were very lucky, prisoners. Moreover, since there was usually enough time between raids on any given city to repair some of the damage, German war production actually continued to rise until late 1944. The theory of strategic bombardment was sound, but the practice was a very expensive aerial equivalent of trench warfare.

German war production was actually hit at least as hard by American bombers that flew by day and aimed at specific industrial targets, although the US Eighth Air Force also suffered huge casualties. But in the war against Japan, where the US Air Force used huge B-29 bombers and more "British" tactics and the air defenses were poor, American casualties were low and the firestorms were more frequent. Soon after Dresden, on March 9, 1945, Gen. Curtis E. LeMay ordered the first mass low-level night raid on Tokyo, using incendiary bombs. "The area attacked was . . . four miles by three . . . with 103,000 inhabitants to the square mile . . . 267,171 buildings were destroyed—about one fourth of the total in Tokyo—and 1,008,000 persons were rendered homeless. In some of the smaller canals the water was actually boiling."[16]

By 1945, strategic bombardment in Japan was actually producing the long-predicted results: "The Twentieth [US] Air Force was destroying cities at . . . [a] cost to Japan [that] was fifty times the cost to us," reported Gen. "Hap" Arnold, head of the US Army Air Force.[17] But it wasn't enough to force a surrender. A full-scale invasion of the Japanese home islands, costing millions more lives, would still have been necessary, if an almost magical American weapon had not broken the spell imposed on the Japanese government by total war.

"Death, the Destroyer of Worlds"

I saw a perfectly outlined city, clear in every detail, coming in. The city was roughly about four miles in diameter: by that time we were at our bombing altitude of thirty-two thousand feet. The navigator came up—looking over my shoulder he said: "Yes, that's Hiroshima, there's no doubt about it." We were so well on the target that the bombardier says: "I can't do anything, there's nothing to do." He says: "It's just sitting there."

Col. Paul Tibbetts, *Enola Gay* pilot

The Manhattan Project to produce a US atomic bomb was launched in June 1942 after warnings from refugee scientists that Germany was working on one. It wasn't, in fact, but the British were certainly thinking about it (they and the Canadians both contributed to the Manhattan Project after 1942), and both the Russians and the Japanese had rudimentary nuclear weapons programs by 1944.[18] And although Germany never took that road, it was developing the ancestors of the cruise missiles (10,500 V-1 "flying bombs" launched against Britain in 1944) and the long-range ballistic missiles (1,115 V-2 missiles on London) that are the main ways of delivering nuclear weapons today. Terrified that the enemy would get them first, most of the relevant scientists everywhere smothered their misgivings and agreed to work on these projects.

Even so, by the time the Manhattan Project scientists moved to the New Mexico desert to test the first atomic bomb in July 1945, some were having second thoughts. Germany was defeated and nobody thought Japan was close to being able to make its own bomb. But it was too late to change their minds. At 5:50 in the morning of July 16, the test went off perfectly, and they saw what they had done. Despite all their calculations, they were stunned.

> We knew the world would not be the same. A few people laughed. A few people cried. Most people were silent. I remembered a line from the Hindu scripture—the Bhagavad Gita. Vishnu is trying to persuade the prince that he should do his duty and to impress him, takes on his multi-armed form and says, "Now I am become Death, the destroyer of worlds." I suppose we all felt that, one way or another.
>
> Robert Oppenheimer, leader of the scientific team at Los Alamos

At the time, the military really saw the atomic bomb as just a more cost-effective way of performing a task that was already a central part of strategy: destroying cities. At a total cost of $2 billion, it was far cheaper than Bomber Command or the Eighth Air Force, and more reliable to boot. On August 6, 1945, Colonel Tibbetts's crew dropped the weapon on Hiroshima, and seventy thousand people were killed in less than five minutes by a single aircraft carrying a single bomb. Afterward, he said, "I couldn't see any city down there, but what I saw was a tremendous area covered by—the only way I could describe it is—a boiling black mass."

It was as if the sun had crashed and exploded. Yellow fireballs were splashing down. [Afterward, on the riverbank], there were so many injured people that there was almost no room to walk. This was only a mile from where the bomb fell. People's clothes had been blown off and their bodies burned by the heat rays. They looked as if they had strips of rags hanging from them. They had water blisters which had already burst, and their skins hung in tatters. I saw people whose intestines were hanging out of their bodies. Some had lost their eyes. Some had their backs torn open so you could see their backbones inside. They were all asking for water.

Mrs. Ochi

If I were given a similar situation in which this country was at war, risking its future, the circumstances being as they were at that time, I don't think I would hesitate one minute to do it over.

Col. Paul Tibbetts

Firestorm cloud over Hiroshima, near local noon, August 6, 1945

A Huge Problem

Col. Tibbetts notwithstanding, war between the great powers is clearly nearing the end of the road. Small countries and non-state groups can still achieve some of their political goals through organized violence, but the great powers will literally be destroyed by it if they cannot break the habit.

Two perhaps small consolations: first, they have never before managed to abstain from fighting each other for so long. And second, as a result of the two world wars, a majority of people everywhere have ceased to see war as glorious, and have instead come to see it as a huge problem.

CHAPTER 8

A Short History of Nuclear War
1945–1990

Cultural Lag

> I'm not saying we wouldn't get our hair mussed, Mister President, but I do say not more than ten or twenty million dead depending on the breaks.
>
> General "Buck" Turgidson (George C. Scott) in Stanley Kubrick's 1963 film *Dr. Strangelove, or: How I Learned to Stop Worrying and Love the Bomb.*

Kubrick intended General Turgidson as a caricature of General Curtis E. LeMay, long-serving commander of the US Air Force's Strategic Air Command (SAC), who really did want a nuclear war. "LeMay believed that ultimately we're going to have to confront these people with nuclear weapons, and by God, we'd better do it when we have greater superiority than we will have in the future," explained former US Defense Secretary Robert S. McNamara in the 2003 documentary film "Fog of War." For LeMay, nuclear weapons had not changed anything fundamental: he thought that a seventeen-to-one US "advantage" over the Soviet Union in the number of nuclear weapons (in the early 1960s) was a useful strategic asset. He was a victim of cultural lag.

The most dangerous part of the Cold War was the early years, when men like LeMay still occupied positions of power. They were gradually succeeded by people who grasped the basic concept of deterrence, and the world became a somewhat safer place—but it remains a seriously dangerous place.

Nuclear weapons have dominated strategic thinking in the great powers for seventy-five years, yet we know practically nothing about how they would actually work in war when used in large numbers. Two quite small ones were dropped on Japanese cities in 1945, and none have been used in war since. It means that strategists discussing nuclear war are like virgins discussing sex: they have theories and even doctrines about nuclear war, but they do not *know* how it would work, except that it would be very bad. They are equally uncertain about the psychological effects, the electromagnetic effects, and the climate effects. But all the useful evidence we have comes from the forty-five-year confrontation between the United States and the Soviet Union (1945–1990) that is known as the Cold War.

The writer . . . is not for the moment concerned about who will win the next war in which atomic bombs are used. Thus far the chief purpose of our military establishment has been to win wars. From now on its chief purpose must be to avert them. It can have almost no other useful purpose.

Bernard Brodie, 1946[1]

Bernard Brodie had just joined the Institute of International Studies at Yale University when the first atomic bomb fell on Hiroshima. Much of the American academic community fantasized about creating a "world government" to prevent nuclear war, but Brodie and a small group of colleagues who knew that wasn't going to happen had begun working out the rules for survival in a world of stubbornly independent nation-states armed with nuclear weapons. In two conferences in September and November 1945, and in innumerable private arguments, they created the theory of nuclear deterrence—complete, definitive, and beyond argument.

"Everything about the atomic bomb is overshadowed by the fact that it exists and that its destructive power is fantastically great," Brodie wrote. There could be no effective defense against atomic weapons, since all defense in aerial warfare works by attrition, and if only a small number of nuclear weapons got through, the destruction would be utterly unacceptable. On their single best day, British defenses against V-1 cruise missiles aimed at London in 1944 shot down 97 out of 101. But, he pointed out, if the four exceptions had been atomic bombs, "London survivors would not have considered the record good."

Moreover, there was a limited number of targets in any country, mostly cities, that were worth using a nuclear weapon on, and the destruction of those targets would effectively amount to the destruction of the society. Beyond a certain point, therefore, the relative numbers of nuclear weapons possessed by each side did not matter: "If 2,000 bombs in the hands of either party is enough to destroy entirely the economy of the other, the fact that one side has 6,000 and the other 2,000 will be of relatively small significance."[2]

The only sane military policy was therefore deterrence. Actually using nuclear weapons to attack a nuclear-armed enemy was pointless, since each side "must fear retaliation, [and] the fact that it destroys the opponent's cities some hours or even days before its own are destroyed may avail it little . . ." The main goal of military preparations in peacetime should be to ensure that a country's nuclear weapons systems will survive a nuclear attack, by dispersing them, hiding them, and/or digging them in. The only source of safety against a nuclear attack is a guaranteed ability to retaliate with nuclear weapons.[3]

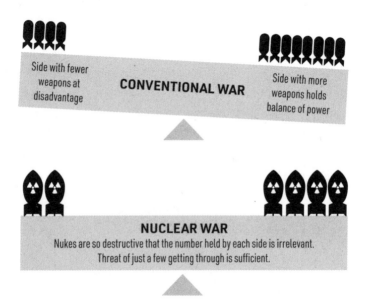

Side with fewer weapons at disadvantage

CONVENTIONAL WAR

Side with more weapons holds balance of power

NUCLEAR WAR
Nukes are so destructive that the number held by each side is irrelevant.
Threat of just a few getting through is sufficient.

There was nothing important left to add. By February 1946, Bernard Brodie and his colleagues had defined the terms on which the peace might be kept in a nuclear-armed world until, someday, the international system that breeds war could somehow be changed. But nobody in power was listening to this little band of young civilians who dared to make policy proposals on military affairs.

To be fair, the US government didn't have to take Brodie's advice in 1946. It was still a conventionally armed world with just one nuclear power, the United States, so deterrence was a one-way street. Indeed, the US government and its European allies saw the American nuclear monopoly as a cheap solution to the West's military security problems. As the United States and the Soviet Union drifted from being wartime allies into a postwar confrontation, the Russians built up their conventional forces in Europe, but the US just built more and more atomic bombs. When the Russians tested their own atomic bomb in 1949, the US doubled down and developed far more powerful hydrogen bombs (thermonuclear weapons). Right through the 1950s the United States had at least a ten-to-one lead over the Soviet Union in nuclear weapons, and it said publicly and repeatedly that it would use nuclear weapons first, directly on Soviet cities, in response to any unacceptable Soviet act.

> Basically, American nuclear policy has been a stated policy of war-fighting with nuclear weapons from the beginning.
> Robert McNamara, US Secretary of Defense, 1961–68[4]

US Secretary of State John Foster Dulles formally enshrined this policy in the doctrine of "massive retaliation" in a speech of January 1954, announcing that the United States would "depend primarily upon a great capacity to retaliate, instantly, by means and at places of our own choosing." Retaliate with the massive use of American nuclear weapons on the Soviet homeland, that is, in response to any Soviet military operation, even a nonnuclear one, that threatened American interests anywhere in the world.

MASSIVE RETALIATION
Immediate overwhelming nuclear response to an attack or threat, whether nuclear or nonnuclear

MINIMUM DETERRENCE
Possessing no more nuclear force than needed to deter nuclear attack; a policy of "No First Use"

It was the exact opposite of the policy of "minimum deterrence" advocated by Bernard Brodie and his colleagues, many of whom were now working as civilian defense analysts at the RAND (Research and Development Corporation) think tank in Santa Monica, California, which was founded and supported by the US Air Force. They were rightly convinced that once the Soviet Union achieved the ability to deliver a quite limited number of thermonuclear weapons on US cities, it simply wouldn't matter that America had a lot more of them, and in 1957 they were afraid that the Russians were nearing that goal. So they persuaded their superiors to warn General LeMay, still running Strategic Air Command, that the growing Soviet bomber fleet might "Pearl Harbor" SAC on the ground.

LeMay wasn't at all worried. He simply replied that US reconnaissance planes were flying secret missions over Soviet territory twenty-four hours a day.

> If I see the Russians are amassing their planes for an attack, I'm going to knock the shit out of them before they take off the ground. I don't care [if it's not national policy]. It's my policy. That's what I'm going to do.
>
> Gen. Curtis LeMay[5]

There is no reason to doubt that LeMay would have done a thorough job—nor that he would have finished the job by destroying most Soviet cities at the same time, since this sort of thing is bound to leave a grudge and no one would want the Russians coming back later for revenge. It is not clear whether he would have apologized if (a) it subsequently became clear that his intelligence people had misinterpreted Soviet movements and they weren't really planning an attack after all, or (b) the whole world went dark and cold.

As the 1950s neared their end, however, the civilian authorities in Washington were getting anxious about the implications of US strategy. As President Dwight Eisenhower said in 1957, "You can't have this kind of war. There just aren't enough bulldozers to scrape the bodies off the streets."[6] One year later, John Foster Dulles went to the Pentagon and formally told the Joint Chiefs of Staff that he was abandoning the policy of massive retaliation.[7]

However, the Eisenhower administration also rejected any suggestion that it should build up US conventional forces in order to fight the wars that it no longer thought could be deterred by massive retaliation. Eisenhower simply ignored SAC's blatant manipulation of intelligence reports to predict a looming "bomber gap" in the Soviet favor from 1955 to 1957, and then an equally mythical "missile gap" from 1957 to 1960. A former career soldier, wise in the ways of the armed services, Eisenhower knew that LeMay was just trying to blackmail him into giving SAC more bombers and missiles. He saw no likely major war on the horizon and simply refused to embark on any kind of crash program to build up further a military establishment that was already terrifying enough to the Soviets for any practical purposes. After all, by 1960 the US had six or seven thousand thermonuclear bombs, all of them dozens of times more powerful than the Hiroshima-scale bombs.[8]

> No country without an atom bomb could properly consider
> itself independent.
>
> Charles de Gaulle, President of France, 1968[9]

During the frantic wartime drive to develop atomic bombs
before (so they feared) the Germans got them, Britain and
Canada had voluntarily merged their considerable resources
of scientific talent, technology, and uranium ore with the
US-based Manhattan Project, but there had been no agreement
about sharing the actual nuclear weapons that emerged from
that project. Naturally, the US government had no intention of
sharing them—which produced markedly different responses
in the other two countries. Canada, despite the significant part
it had played in the war, had no pretensions to a global military
role, so it decided virtually without debate that nuclear weapons
were irrelevant to its security. Britain looked at the Soviet army
sitting in the middle of Germany, less than four hundred miles
away, and concluded that it urgently needed nuclear weapons
of its own in case things went wrong.

France reached exactly the same conclusion and launched
its own nuclear weapons program. Once the Chinese Communist regime fell out with Moscow in the late 1950s, it, too,
launched a nuclear weapons program designed to deter a Soviet
nuclear attack—and in every case, these were "minimum deterrent" forces. None of these nations had the ability to place a
nuclear weapon on every missile silo and small town in the
Soviet Union, as the United States had, but they did not think
it necessary.

The French spoke of being able to "tear an arm off the Soviet
bear." The British had an explicit "Moscow criterion" for their

nuclear forces: so long as Britain could obliterate Moscow, they calculated, the Russians would probably not use nuclear weapons against British targets. But both countries also privately saw their nukes as a way of ensuring that Washington's nerve did not fail in the face of a Soviet conventional attack in Europe. Despite all America's promises of "massive retaliation," it might decide on the day to let western Europe go under rather than launch a nuclear war in which American cities would also burn. Independent British and French nuclear forces guaranteed that that wouldn't happen. To ensure that their missiles couldn't be eliminated in a surprise first strike, both countries also emulated the American example and sent some of their missiles out to sea in submarines.

During the 1980s, both Britain and France embarked on an expansion of their nuclear forces, giving them the ability to destroy close to a thousand targets each. China, while showing more restraint on the numbers issue, sent some of its nuclear missiles out to sea in submarines as soon as possible, as a policy of minimum deterrence dictates. Israel, whose first nuclear weapons were probably built in the mid-1960s, did not put any of them into submarines until much later, because it had no reason to fear that it might lose its weapons to an Arab surprise attack. No Arab country then or now possesses nuclear weapons, so Israel was free to pursue an undeclared strategy of "massive retaliation": all Arab states knew that an Israeli military defeat in a conventional war could trigger the use of Israeli nuclear weapons. Anecdotal evidence strongly suggests that Israel was actively preparing to use its nuclear weapons during the first few panic-stricken days of its 1973 war with Egypt and Syria.

The signature of the Nuclear Non-Proliferation Treaty of 1968, in which the five declared nuclear weapons powers agreed not to transfer their weapons to other countries, and over a hundred other countries agreed not to develop nuclear weapons themselves, put an end to this twenty-year period during which the number of countries possessing nuclear weapons jumped from one to six. Israel just kept quiet about it, and thirty years passed before another country openly went nuclear.

The Fallacy of Limited Nuclear War

> I thought they were the most dangerous, depraved, essentially monstrous people. They really had constructed a doomsday machine.
>
> Daniel Ellsberg, 1961

When the Kennedy administration came to office in 1961 (much helped electorally by the "missile gap" myth), it brought a whole group of analysts from RAND to the Department of Defense. One of them, Daniel Ellsberg, was shown the first Single Integrated Operational Plan (SIOP), which allocated targets for nuclear weapons among all the various branches of the US armed forces. He was shocked: SAC's only war plan was to launch all US nuclear weapons at once against every city and significant military target in the Soviet Union and China, and most of those in eastern Europe as well. Nothing would be held back for a second strike, there was no way to leave China and the Soviet-occupied "satellite"' countries in eastern Europe out, even if they were not involved—and the strike would kill between 360 and 425 million people, more than one tenth of the world's population at the time. Since every branch of the US armed forces wanted to get its own nukes on Moscow, the Soviet capital would be hit by 170 different atomic and hydrogen bombs.[10]

Robert McNamara, Kennedy's secretary of defense, had the same SIOP briefing as Ellsberg and was similarly appalled, but SAC had foreseen that and came up with a new idea less offensive to civilian sensibilities. In the Air Force's new scenario, the United States, unable to stop a Soviet attack in western Europe with conventional forces, strikes at Soviet bomber fields, missile sites, and submarine pens with nuclear weapons, but avoids hitting Soviet cities and holds part of its force in reserve. The Soviets strike back but avoid attacking US cities. Since the United States launched first, it wins the "counterforce" exchange and then tells the Soviets to surrender or it will pick off their cities one by one. Moscow surrenders, and the total cost of the war is "only" three million American lives and five million Soviet lives.

Theatrical release poster for *Duck and Cover* dir. Anthony Rizzo, 1952

McNamara was sucked in by this "counterforce" strategy, which sounded significantly less crazy than the existing SIOP, and told SAC to go ahead and develop a doctrine that "would permit controlled response and negotiating pauses" in the event of thermonuclear war. By the end of the year, the revised US strategic plan, SIOP-63, allowed the commander to reprogram the targets of American missiles on short notice and to fire them singly or in small numbers (rather than in minimum batches of fifty). It became theoretically possible for the United States to fight a "limited," no-cities nuclear war—*if the Russians agreed*.[11] McNamara didn't really trust this strategy—he privately advised both President Kennedy and President Johnson that they should never use nuclear weapons first under any circumstances—but officially the new SIOP assumed that restraint and rationality could prevail even after nuclear weapons began to explode over the homelands. Events soon demonstrated how far removed that was from reality.

Cuban Missile Crisis

Nuclear warhead bunker under construction in San Cristobal, Cuba, October 23, 1962

In late 1961 the Soviet leader, Nikita Khrushchev, realized that the new American reconnaissance satellites had exposed his claim to possess a large intercontinental ballistic missile (ICBM) force as a mere bluff. Feeling embarrassed and vulnerable, he took the gamble in 1962 of secretly deploying shorter-range missiles on the territory of his new ally, Cuba, in order to put American cities within range of a substantial Soviet missile force and thus close the strategic gap.

The US discovered the missiles, and the Cuban Missile Crisis erupted. The United States declared a blockade of Cuba, and began preparations for an invasion if Khrushchev didn't withdraw his missiles. And faced with a real crisis, nobody paid the least attention to the idea of a "counterforce" or limited nuclear war.

The Soviet side was much weaker, but at least a few of Khrushchev's bombers and missiles would get through to devastate American cities no matter what the United States did. Instead, everybody fled back to the relative sanity of Brodie's original deterrent formula. On October 22, Kennedy declared that the United States would regard "any nuclear missile launched from Cuba against any nation in the western hemisphere as an attack by the Soviet Union on the United States *requiring a full retaliatory response upon the Soviet Union* [emphasis added]."[12]

But there was still some time left, President Kennedy believed, for American intelligence sources were telling him that the Soviet missiles in Cuba still lacked their nuclear warheads. Kennedy therefore concentrated on intercepting Soviet ships that might be carrying the warheads to Cuba, while pushing ahead with the plan to invade the island if Moscow did not back down. And after a terrifying thirteen days, Moscow did back down. Khrushchev sent a letter to Kennedy offering to withdraw the Soviet missiles from Cuba in return for an American promise not to invade the island and to withdraw similar American missiles from Turkey a few months later.

Nobody on the American side realized at the time just how close they had come to a nuclear war. If Khrushchev had not sent his proposal for a compromise, the US invasion of Cuba would probably have gone ahead, but everybody in Washington assumed that there would be at least a few more steps in the dance before nuclear weapons were actually used. Thirty years later, Robert McNamara found out that everybody in Washington had been dead wrong.

It wasn't until January, 1992, in a meeting chaired by Fidel Castro in Havana, Cuba, that I learned that 162 nuclear warheads including 90 tactical warheads were on the island at this critical moment of the crisis. I couldn't believe what I was hearing, and . . . I said, ". . . Mr President [Castro], I have three questions to you. Number one, did you know the nuclear warheads were there? Number two, if you did, would you have recommended to Khrushchev in the face of a US attack that he use them? Number three, if he used them, what would have happened to Cuba?"

He said, "Number one, I knew they were there. Number two . . . I *did* recommend to Khrushchev that they be used. Number three, what would have happened to Cuba? It would have been totally destroyed."

That's how close we were . . . and he went on to say, "Mr. McNamara, if you and President Kennedy had been in a similar situation, that's what you would have done." I said, "Mr. President, I hope to God we would not have done it. Pull the temple down on our own heads? My God!"

Robert McNamara, from *The Fog of War*

Threatening to pull the temple down on your own head and everybody else's is the very essence of nuclear deterrence, but there is a measure of reassurance to be had from these events. The Cuban crisis demonstrated that the penalties for miscalculation in a nuclear confrontation are so huge that political leaders become extremely cautious and conservative in their actions; people *do* recognize the difference between simulation and reality.

On the other hand, it also demonstrated that intelligence will always be imperfect and that seemingly rational decisions may actually be fatal. If the United States had invaded Cuba to deal with the missiles before they were operational (as it thought), its Marines would have been obliterated on the beaches by tactical nuclear missiles launched by local Soviet commanders who had been pre-authorized to act without reference back to Moscow, and World War III would have begun. President Kennedy later estimated that the chance of the Cuban crisis ending in a nuclear war was one in three.[13]

The Cuban Missile Crisis ought to have ended for good the notion of a limited nuclear war in American strategic circles: nobody seriously considered "signaling their resolve" with a few selective nuclear strikes when they were immersed in a real crisis. Nevertheless, the next twenty years of American nuclear war policy were largely dominated by the continuing split between the believers who wanted to make nuclear weapons usable in limited wars and those who had finally lost the faith.

CAMP ONE	CAMP TWO
No lessons to be learned from the Cuba Missile Crisis. Limited Nuclear War is possible: a tactical first strike guarantees the surrender of an enemy unwilling to endanger its population in the escalation.	Limited Nuclear War is a mirage: there are too many unknowns. The Cuba crisis proved intelligence is imperfect and that the enemy is not predictable. Minimum Deterrence is therefore the only sane option.

Engineers or Soldiers?

By the early 1980s US doctrine for fighting a nuclear war had become a structure of such baroque and self-referential complexity that it had only a distant relationship with the real world. It was almost as separated from reality as the missile crews who sat the long watches underground in their reinforced concrete command bunkers.

Q. How would you feel if you ever had to do it for real?
A. Well, we're trained so highly in our recurrent training that we take every month . . . that if we actually had to launch the missiles, it would be an almost automatic thing.
Q. You wouldn't be thinking about it at the time?
A. There wouldn't be time for any reflection until after we turned the keys . . .
Q. Would there be reflection then, do you think?
A. I should think so, yes.

Conversation with Minuteman ICBM crew commander,
Whiteman Air Force Base, 1982

Minuteman crew member during "personnel reliability" testing

As late as 1945, the bomber crews could see the cities burning beneath them (though not the people), but a Minuteman launch crew never sees its targets, which are six thousand miles away. The young man quoted above wore a label on his pocket that said "combat crew," and he would probably have been killed if there had been an "exchange" of nuclear-tipped ballistic missiles, but he was not a warrior. His job, in practice, closely resembled that of the duty engineer at a nuclear power plant, and he passed the long hours of his watch working on a correspondence course for an MBA. Not a lot like your average infantryman—but then nuclear war is not really a military enterprise in any recognizable sense.

Star Wars

By the early 1980s, the five nuclear powers had accumulated a total of over 2,500 land-based ballistic missiles, well over a thousand submarine-launched ballistic missiles, and thousands of aircraft capable of carrying nuclear bombs, plus land-, sea-, and air-launched cruise missiles and a wide range of "battlefield" nuclear weapons. There were more than fifty thousand nuclear warheads in the world—and then president Ronald Reagan introduced the concept of the Strategic Defense Initiative ("Star Wars").

The promoters of Star Wars never believed that it could completely shield the United States from a nuclear attack, for Bernard Brodie's 1946 observation remained true: all air (and space) defense operates on the principle of attrition, which means that some portion of the attacking weapons will always get through. If they are nuclear weapons, even a very small fraction is too many. But space-based US defenses *might* eventually be able to cope with a ragged retaliatory strike if the Soviet Union had already been devastated by a largely successful American first strike.

President Reagan himself never realized what the people who sold him on the Star Wars concept were really after. It wasn't blanket national protection against nuclear attack, but a partial defense for the missile fields and other strategic installations from which the United States might one day try to wage and win a limited nuclear war. It was the same old game they had been playing for twenty years, but they appealed to his genuine aversion to nuclear weapons, and he fell for it because of his longing for a magical release from the threat of nuclear war. The Russian leadership understood very well what Reagan's secretary of defense, Caspar Weinberger, and the Cold Warriors around him were up to, and they were not happy about it.

> On the face of it, laymen may find it even attractive as [President Reagan] speaks about what seem to be defensive measures . . . In fact the strategic offensive forces of the United States will continue to be developed and upgraded at full tilt [with the aim] of acquiring a first nuclear strike capability . . . [It is] a bid to disarm the Soviet Union.
>
> Soviet leader Yuri Andropov, 1983[14]

End of Evil Empire

The Cold War never quite turned hot. Promising changes began in the Soviet Union after the death of long-ruling dictator Leonid Brezhnev in 1982, and by 1985 a radical reformer called Mikhail Gorbachev came to power. Ronald Reagan's desire to end the threat of nuclear war was equally genuine, and at the Reykjavik summit in 1986 he horrified his advisers by proposing that both countries get rid of all their ballistic missiles. Basing nuclear deterrence only on relatively slow-moving bombers and cruise missiles would make the world a safer place, he argued.

That particular initiative was shot down by both men's advisers, but on Gorbachev's first visit to the US in 1987, the two men signed the Intermediate Nuclear Forces treaty, ending the panic over the introduction of a new generation of nuclear missiles in Europe. By the time Reagan visited Moscow in June, 1988, he declared that "of course" the Cold War was over, and that his "evil empire" talk was from "another time." Even before the fall of the Berlin Wall in the following year, the United States and the Soviet Union had ceased to be strategic adversaries.

So the first long military confrontation between two nuclear-armed powers ended peacefully, but it offered no guarantees for the future. It could have been just forty years of dumb luck, for it came close to the actual use of nuclear weapons several times, and new technologies continually unleashed new instabilities into the system.

Moreover, only at the very end did everyone find out what would have happened if all those weapons had ever been used.

Reagan and Gorbachev meet for the first time in Geneva, November 1985

> We have, by slow and imperceptible steps, been construct-
> ing a Doomsday Machine. Until recently and then, only by
> accident—no one even noticed. And we have distributed its
> triggers all over the Northern Hemisphere.
>
> Carl Sagan[15]

In 1971 a small group of scientists who had gathered to analyze *Mariner 9*'s observations of Mars found that the entire planet was covered by an immense dust storm that lasted three months. With nothing better to do, they passed the time by calculating how such a long-lasting dust cloud would alter conditions on the Martian surface. Answer: it would lower the ground temperature drastically.

The dust storm was still raging, so they then examined meteorological records to see if exploding volcanoes here on Earth (which boost relatively small amounts of dust into the upper atmosphere) produced similar effects. Every time a major volcano has gone off, they found, there has been a small drop in the average global temperature lasting a year or more.

This was interesting—and the surface of Mars was still obscured—so they went on to examine the consequences of stray asteroids colliding with the earth and blasting vast quantities of dust into the atmosphere. That had happened numerous times in the long past and there was evidence that at least one of these collisions resulted in temporary but huge climate changes that caused mass extinctions of living things.

Then the dust storm on Mars ended, they analyzed *Mariner 9*'s data, and they went their separate ways. But they stayed in touch (they called themselves the TTAPS, after the first letters of their last names) and kept working on the new problem they had stumbled on. Twelve years later, in 1983, they published their results.

A major nuclear exchange, the TTAPS group concluded, would cover at least the northern hemisphere, and perhaps the entire planet, with a pall of smoke and dust that would plunge the surface into virtual darkness for up to six months. In the continental interiors, the surface temperature would drop by as much as 40 degrees C (below the freezing point in any season) for a similar period. And when enough of the dust and soot particles drifted down from the stratosphere to let the sun's light back in, the destruction of the ozone layer by thermonuclear fireballs would let two or three times as much ultraviolet light reach the surface, causing blindness or lethal sunburn in exposed humans.[16]

Everybody already knew that a major nuclear war would instantly kill several hundred million people in the NATO and Warsaw Pact countries and destroy most of the world's industry and its artistic, scientific, and architectural heritage. Fallout and the disruption of northern hemisphere agriculture would cause hundreds of millions more deaths from famine and disease in the aftermath. But the prospect of a "nuclear winter" was much worse.

Now we knew that the cold and the dark would persist worldwide for half a year after a major nuclear war, killing off entire species of animals and plants already weakened by high doses of radioactivity—and that when the gloom finally cleared, ultraviolet radiation, starvation, and disease would account for many others. In April 1983, a symposium of forty distinguished biologists concluded:

> Species extinction could be expected for most tropical plants and animals, and for most terrestrial vertebrates of north temperate regions, a large number of plants, and numerous freshwater and some marine organisms . . . It is clear that the ecosystem effects alone resulting from a large-scale thermonuclear war could be enough to destroy the current civilization in at least the Northern Hemisphere. Coupled with the direct casualties of perhaps two billion people, the combined intermediate and long-term effects of nuclear war suggest that eventually there might be no human survivors in the Northern Hemisphere . . .
>
> In almost any realistic case involving nuclear exchanges between the superpowers, global environmental changes sufficient to cause an extinction event equal to or more severe than that at the close of the Cretaceous when the dinosaurs and many other species died out are likely. In that event, the possibility of the extinction of Homo Sapiens cannot be excluded.
>
> Paul R. Ehrlich et al.[17]

How many nuclear weapons would be needed to produce these effects? It depends what kind of war you are fighting. If it's the sort of "limited" nuclear war, beloved of the theorists, where each side only attacks the other side's airfields, missile silos, etc., and avoids cities, quite a lot. It would take up to two or three thousand high-yield ground-bursts to produce a nuclear winter. But the total nuclear weapons stockpile of the United States and the Soviet Union in the mid-1980s was about thirteen thousand megatons, which was ample to fight that kind of war.

The threshold is much lower for a war in which cities are hit, because the millions of tons of soot given off by burning cities would be a very powerful screening agent. As few as one hundred one-megaton airbursts over one hundred cities could be too much.[18] Even India and Pakistan are approaching that threshold, and it is unrealistic to imagine that cities would really be spared in a nuclear war: too many of the vital leadership, command and control, and industrial targets are embedded in them. Cities would be struck, and they would burn.

There was a great deal of research done on "nuclear winter" in the later 1980s, and the hypothesis held up despite major official efforts to discredit it. In 1990 the TTAPS group summarized the research in *Science*,[19] and reported that "the basic physics of nuclear winter has been reaffirmed through several authoritative international technical assessments and numerous individual scientific investigations." Little further research has been done on nuclear winter since 1990, due to the sudden loss of interest in the subject of nuclear war after the collapse of the Soviet Union.

Our Way of Thinking

It is now three quarters of a century since any great power has directly fought any other, the longest interlude between such events since the emergence of the modern state system in the mid-1600s. But no great power has renounced war as an instrument of policy, and war between great powers, in our technological era, probably means nuclear war. There will be new confrontations between the great powers in the decades and centuries to come, and they will doubtless involve the same sorts of doctrinal mismatch, cultural misunderstanding, and technological hubris that marked the first one.

We have arrived at the dilemma that has lain in wait for us from the start: war is deeply ingrained in our culture, but it is lethally incompatible with an advanced technological civilization. Albert Einstein saw it clearly in 1945: "Everything has changed, except our way of thinking."

"Everything has changed, except our way of thinking." Albert Einstein.

CHAPTER 9

Trifurcation: Nuclear, Conventional, Terrorist

New Categories

> If we employ [nuclear weapons] on the enemy, we invite retaliation, shock, horror, and a cycle of retaliation with an end that is most difficult to foresee . . . We are flung into a straitjacket of rationality, which prevents us from lashing out at the enemy . . . Warfare must be returned to its traditional place as politics pursued by other means.
>
> William Kaufmann, RAND analyst, 1955[1]

There used to be only one kind of war. It was conducted by states, it involved armies, and it had strategies that served political ends. There were other kinds of violence as well, from popular revolts to mere banditry, but the distinction was clear. And then suddenly, after 1945, there were three kinds of war: the nuclear wars that all great powers had to prepare for but never fight, the guerrilla wars and terrorism that have captured and held the public's attention for the past seventy-five years—and, of course, the "conventional" wars continuing to flourish beneath and beyond the nuclear stalemate.

The category of "conventional war" did not exist before 1945, because all wars were conventional. For the great powers, it should have virtually vanished after 1945, because nuclear weapons made war between them even by traditional means—armies fighting other armies, taking and holding territory—unthinkably dangerous. Yet the great powers still dwelt in an international system that took the possibility of war as a given, and each government was served by large and powerful institutions whose purpose was to prepare for and, if necessary, fight wars. It was an insoluble dilemma, so they never solved it.

The two victorious countries that emerged from the Second World War as "superpowers," the United States and the Soviet Union, divided Europe, the center of world power for the previous three centuries, into spheres of influence whose borders ran roughly along the line where their armies had halted in 1945. They then identified each other as enemies and entered into a long and dangerous military confrontation. That was perfectly normal, as was the fact that they emphasized their ideological differences to explain, justify, and reinforce a hostility that would have happened anyway. It's unlikely that either superpower ever intended to attack the other, but on average they would then have been about half a century away from the next world war. Depending on how you define a world war.

Shuffling the Pack

We normally count only the two great wars of the twentieth century as "world wars," but they were really just the same old thing with better weapons technologies. Politically, a "world war" is one in which all the great powers of the time are involved. Between 1600 and 1950 all the great powers—that is to say those able to project serious force at a significant distance from their own borders—were European, and they happened to have globe-spanning empires so their wars in this period were fought all over the planet. But geography is not the decisive criterion. What makes it a world war is that all the great powers join together in two great rival alliances, and that the war ends up being about practically everything. At the end of it, the outstanding disputes between the great powers go into the pot and get sorted by the peace settlement.

By this criterion, there have been six world wars in modern history: the Thirty Years' War of 1618–48, the War of the Spanish Succession in 1702–14, the Seven Years' War of 1756–63, the Revolutionary and Napoleonic wars of 1791–1815, and the two that actually bear the name of World War, in 1914–18 and 1939–45. At the time people saw these wars as having "settled" things conclusively, and having defined the relative status of the great powers in the ensuing period of relative peace. What they didn't often notice (because most of them were only alive for one of these events) was that the "world wars" were coming along roughly every half century.

Apart from the long nineteenth-century gap, the great powers have gone to war with each other about every fifty years throughout modern history—and even the "long peace" of the nineteenth century is deceptive. Between 1854 and 1870, right on schedule, every great power fought one or several others: Britain, France, and Turkey against Russia; France and Italy against Austria; Germany against Austria; and then Germany against France. Because all of these wars except the first ended in a decisive victory in no more than six months, they didn't expand in the usual way to include all the great powers. (The longer a war between any two great powers lasts, the likelier it is to drag in the others.)

Nevertheless, this series of smaller wars brought about changes in the international distribution of power just as significant as those normally wrought by world wars. A united Italy and a powerful German empire emerged in the heart of Europe, while the relative decline of Austria was confirmed and

France lost its position as the greatest continental power. The great power system then settled into a long period of peace: the Treaty of Frankfurt in 1871, like the Congress of Vienna in 1815, was followed by four decades in which no European great powers fought each other.

What made this pattern so cyclical? Why did the great powers all go to war roughly every fifty years?

Each world war reshuffles the pack, and then the peace treaty freezes all the border changes and defines the rank of the great powers in the new international pecking order. Peace settlements reflect the real power relationships in the world at the time when they are signed. They are easily enforceable, because the winners have just beaten the losers in war. But as the decades pass, the wealth and population of some powers grow fast while others decline. After half a century, the real power relationships in the world are very different from those prescribed by the last peace settlement. This is when some rising power, frustrated by its allotted place in the existing international system, or some frightened country that fears it is losing too much ground, kicks off the next reshuffle of the pack.

There is no magic in the figure of fifty years. It's simply how long it takes for the realities of power to part company with the relationships reflected by the last peace. Our ability to see the normal historical rhythm is hampered because World War II came only twenty years after World War I, but that is probably due to the fact that the latter was the first *total* war. It therefore ended in a particularly draconian peace treaty, since even the winners had suffered so greatly that they were unnecessarily vengeful. "Tremendous victories make bad peaces," as Guglielmo Ferrero remarked, and indeed the Treaty of Versailles in 1919, with its extreme terms, was an unsustainable distortion of the real power relationships in the world. Germany lost the war, but it was not going to remain inferior in power to France for the next fifty years.

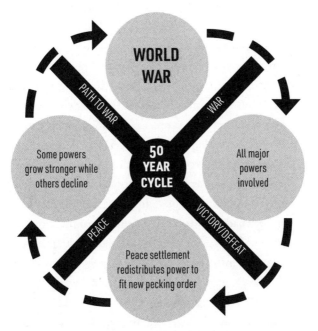

World War II ended in an equally tremendous victory, but the subsequent peace between the great powers has already lasted almost four times as long. The post-1945 settlement did break down more or less on schedule, at the end of the 1980s—but it was replaced peacefully. So why didn't the Cold War end in World War III after fifty years or so?

Foolish or desperate?

> War is nothing more than the continuation of policy by other means.
>
> Karl von Clausewitz[2]

Over the millennia, a large body of beliefs has accumulated about the merciless environment in which states operate. Those who rise to positions of political power know that quarrels settled by law when occurring within a state are frequently settled by war when they occur between states, there being little international law and no international law enforcement. And those who served in the armed forces, even in the late twentieth century, were obliged to believe simultaneously that nuclear weapons had rendered war unthinkable, and that it was still possible.

For more than four decades, an entire working lifetime for a generation of soldiers, there was a sustained attempt to turn Central Europe into a game park where the great powers could preserve an endangered species, conventional war, because the alternative was a return to total war. And it would be a *nuclear* total war, next time. But the line they drew between conventional and nuclear war was an artificial distinction, and a pretty flimsy one.

It has always frightened me to death, ever since I was to command a division in Germany in the late Fifties and the nuclear weapon appeared for the first time as a cotton-wool cloud on the sand table. The assumption that you can control a nuclear war is pure fantasy . . . [The] one thing you can count on is that there will be a very high probability of early and steep escalation into the strategic all-out exchange that nobody wants. So you mustn't use the things.

Gen. Sir John Hackett

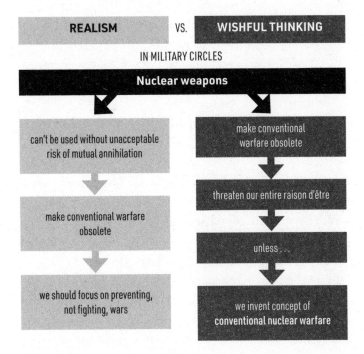

REALISM VS. WISHFUL THINKING

IN MILITARY CIRCLES

Nuclear weapons

can't be used without unacceptable risk of mutual annihilation

make conventional warfare obsolete

make conventional warfare obsolete

threaten our entire raison d'être

we should focus on preventing, not fighting, wars

unless . . .

we invent concept of **conventional nuclear warfare**

The Soviet acquisition of a nuclear capability roughly comparable to that of the United States should have ended the period when Washington saw nuclear strikes as a usable military tool, since both countries would effectively be destroyed in such a war. Yet both sides continued to modernize their conventionally armed troops along the "Central Front" (the East-West German border), and even elaborated theories for how "tactical" nuclear weapons might be used in circumstances short of all-out nuclear war.

There is no such thing as a pre-planned escalation which necessarily must follow in steps, so that it would be first a conventional war and then a nuclear war. This would be very

much against our philosophy of flexible response. Flexible
response means that the enemy faces a completely incalcula-
ble risk. It might even be that we use nuclear weapons from
the outset. If the political decision is made for that, the military is prepared to do it.

Gen. Ferdinand von Senger und Etterlin, commander-in-
chief, Allied Forces Central Europe, 1982

Despite the general's fighting words, the doctrine of *flexible
response* was really an attempt by NATO to keep a war in Europe
at a "conventional" World War II level for at least a little while,
before both sides went nuclear—and in practice the Soviets had
adopted the same policy by 1970. Both sides hoped that, even
after the first relatively low-yield nuclear weapons had been used
in Europe—probably to stop a breakthrough somewhere—they
could still limit escalation beyond "battlefield" nuclear weapons
for at least a few more days before the "strategic" nukes started
destroying cities in the Russian and American homelands.

Were the soldiers who devoted their lives to this enterprise
foolish or just desperate? Some had not yet grasped the truth
that Bernard Brodie articulated in 1945—that their function
now was to avert war, not wage it—but the better informed
knew that nuclear weapons had "changed everything."
However, they were soldiers with orders to guard a border, so
they did the best they could. If the ability to hold two opposing
ideas in mind at the same time and still retain the ability to
function is the mark of a first-rate intelligence (as F. Scott Fitzgerald proposed), then they passed the test.

A "limited" nuclear war on the Central Front would not
only have destroyed most of the armies that were engaged; it
would also have killed millions or tens of millions of civilians
in central Europe in a matter of days. Perhaps it would have

provided a last brief opportunity for reflection and second thoughts before the opponents moved on to "strategic" nuclear weapons and the devastation of the entire northern hemisphere. And perhaps not.

In Wintex '83, one of the last annual NATO command and staff exercises before the Cold War began to shut down, the script had the Warsaw Pact forces crossing the border into West Germany on March 3. On March 8, NATO's commanders requested authority to use their nuclear weapons to stop the Soviet breakthrough, and the first nuclear strike against the Warsaw Pact was ordered on March 9. The conventional war, in this exercise, lasted six days.

Rehearsing for Armageddon: British troops on NATO's exercise Lionheart in Germany, 1984

Not So Conventional

The obsession with nuclear weapons during the Cold War obscured another new reality that had been creeping up on the soldiers, and continues to do so today: even a purely conventional war fought with state-of-the-art weapons has become problematic. The latest generation of weapons—battlefield surveillance systems, weapons with a "one-shot kill capability," swarms of drones and the like—are transforming conventional war, and some theorists even talk about a "revolution in military affairs" (RMA). There is such a thing, no doubt, but not in quite the sense they intend. The real RMA has been the huge increase in the rate of loss of combat systems in battle, partly because the new weapons have become so complex and expensive to build that there are far fewer of them, and partly because they are so lethally good at destroying each other.

Israeli tank crossing the Suez Canal during Arab-Israeli war, October 1973

The last time evenly matched modern armies fought a serious conventional war was almost half a century ago, in the 1973 Middle East war between Israel and two of its Arab neighbors, Egypt and Syria. In that war, the Israelis lost close to half their total stock of tanks to wire-guided anti-tank missiles in less than a week. Similarly, the Israeli Air Force lost over one hundred aircraft out of a total stock of 390 warplanes in the first four days of the war, to Russian-built surface-to-air missiles. Happily for Israel, the United States began a massive airborne resupply operation in the eighth day of the war, flying in many hundreds of tanks, combat aircraft, artillery pieces and TOW anti-tank weapons. Few other countries, however, have instant access to a similar resupply service in the event of war.

Since the Second World War there has also been a drastic shrinkage in the average size of national armed forces worldwide, except where there is a particularly high level of perceived threat, and the main reason is money. There is no point maintaining armies with more manpower than you can afford to equip with state-of-the-art weapons, and most nations cannot justify producing very large numbers of those weapons in peacetime. Virtually unlimited money would become instantly available if the great powers found themselves at war with each other, but it would take time to expand weapons production significantly. A war between NATO and the Warsaw Pact on the "Central Front" in Europe in the 1980s would have been (as soldiers said at the time) a "come as you are" war: both sides would immediately have started losing their major weapons systems like tanks and aircraft at a rate they could not hope to replace.

To grasp the scale of the escalation in cost of military hardware, consider the Spitfire, probably the best fighter in the world when it entered service with the Royal Air Force in 1939. It then cost £5,000 to build: equivalent to the average annual income of about thirty British adults. When its early 1980s replacement, the air defense version of the Tornado, entered service with the Royal Air Force, each one cost £17 million (total annual income of 3,750 Britons). The RAF's most recent acquisition, the American-built F-35B, which carried out its first operational missions in 2019, costs £190 million a copy, including engines and electronics (6,785 Brits' annual income). To put it another way, after allowing for inflation, an F-35B is 225 times as expensive as a Spitfire. No country is 225 times richer than it was at the beginning of World War II, so far fewer weapons can be built. At the height of the Battle of Britain in 1940, Britain was building just over 100 fighters each week. Today the total fighter strength of the RAF is about 120.

The current generation of fighters is much better than those of World War II, of course. They can fly four times as fast and carry five or six times the weight of munitions; they can detect and attack an opponent at a hundred times the range a Spitfire could manage, and their weapons are far more accurate and lethal. But that just makes the problem worse: not only can air forces afford fewer aircraft, but they are going to lose them at a faster rate.

British Spitfire (left) and American F-35B (right)

More recent conventional conflicts have either been between armies using mostly previous-generation weapons, as in the Iran-Iraq war of 1980–88, or showcasing the abilities of a particular weapon, as with the sea-skimming anti-ship missiles used during the Falklands war between Britain and Argentina in 1982, or hopelessly one-sided fights, as with the two wars between the United States and Iraq (1990–91 and 2003). None of them tells us in any detail what would happen if two large military forces, both equipped and trained to the level of the current US armed forces, were to fight each other.

If war had come to Europe in the 1980s, for example, the NATO commander in Europe would have had around three million military personnel (of whom 400,000 were American) under his command, plus another 1.7 million reserves at high readiness. His Soviet counterpart would have had roughly comparable forces, although with rather more tanks. These were the largest mechanized armies anywhere in the world, but they did not remotely compare with the armies deployed by the great powers in the twentieth-century's two world wars. Each day's fighting might easily have seen the destruction of a thousand tanks and several hundred aircraft, and neither side would have been able to replace them quickly. The problem of attrition was already paramount.

> [There might have been] an extraordinarily short burst of mutual wiping out of first-line equipment, leaving the armies dependent on quite simple weapons—a return to an earlier phase of warfare. We had that in 1914: all the sides had gone to war with stocks quite inadequate for the scale of the fighting that took place, and there was then the famous "winter pause" which was partly to lick their wounds . . . and very much to gear up the shell factories. Because the inventory of weapons is so much larger [it would now be] a pause for the replacement of almost everything: tanks, aircraft, missiles, missile launchers, armored vehicles of all sorts . . .
>
> Sir John Keegan, military historian

| Hi-tech new conventional weapons: more lethal and far more expensive | → | each side quickly destroys other's hardware . . . | → | which can't be replaced as fast as it is lost so . . . | → | combatants revert to lower-tech weapons while rebuilding |

All this is assuming, of course, that the "conventional" war lasts considerably longer than the six days of "Wintex '83."

In the mid-1980s, NATO and the Warsaw Pact together, with a combined population of almost a billion people, had enough first-line conventional weapons to equip fewer than ten million troops: under 1 percent of their population. The end of the Cold War in 1988–89 saw a further rapid decline in the size of the armies, driven mainly by a steep fall in mutual threat perception during the 1990s as Russia became democratic, in a ramshackle sort of way. The return to de facto autocracy in Moscow under Vladimir Putin after 1999 did not lead to a renewed arms race, despite the best efforts of the military-industrial complex on both sides, because Russia, shorn of its "satellite" countries and much farther away from the western European heartlands, could no longer be plausibly portrayed to a Western audience as an imminent military threat. On the other hand, a Russian leader seeking a pretext for reassembling the old Russian/Soviet empire could certainly represent NATO's eastward advance to his own people as a threat that justified taking some or all of the countries immediately west of Russia back under Moscow's control, and in due course that misfortune came to pass.

It would have been unthinkable to rebuff the requests of former Warsaw Pact countries to join NATO in the 1990s, since their anxieties about a return of Russian expansionism arose from a much more recent and vivid trauma than comparable Russian obsessions about the Mongol conquest (1237), Muslim slave raids (last Tatar raid on Moscow 1769), Napoleon (1812), and Hitler (1941). Everybody needs reassurance, but the newly democratic eastern European countries had just emerged from half a century of strict Russian/Soviet control, and they were entitled to seek guarantees for their security even if Russia was behaving well at that point.

In terms of real military security, the whole argument about where NATO's eastern boundary should be is of little importance, for nobody really imagines that a potential future confrontation between NATO and Russia would be decided by tank armies racing across the steppes. It's hard even to imagine what the purpose of such a war might be: Russia has nothing of interest to the West that could not be more easily acquired by simply paying for it, and the idea that the Russians might invade NATO countries flies in the face of reality. Once upon a time it was marginally plausible, but not now.

In the mid-1980s the total population of NATO members was about 675 million and the Warsaw Pact's was around 390 million, but since almost half of NATO's population was far away across the Atlantic, each side did pose a genuine threat to the other, in terms of the strength they had on the ground in Europe. By 2020 the Warsaw Pact was long gone and all the former east European satellites had joined NATO. Even the Soviet Union's fifteen republics had broken apart, leaving 145 million relatively impoverished Russians alone to face a NATO alliance now drawing on the resources of 870 million people. The NATO-Warsaw Pact population ratio used to be about three-to-two; now the NATO-Russia ratio is more like five-to-one. In terms of wealth, it's around fifteen-to-one.

The location of NATO's eastern border and its distance from Moscow are red herrings. The relatively sparse military forces near the frontiers on either side are merely trip wires, and any open NATO-Russian conflict would quickly migrate to the nuclear strategic level (although one hopes not to the actual use of nuclear weapons). At that level, it doesn't really matter where the missiles are based, and they are certainly unlikely to be based close to vulnerable borders. Despite all the recent excitements, it remains hard to write a convincing scenario for a full-scale, continent-wide conventional war in Europe today.

Russian and NATO generals do what they can to stir up interest in the 'threats' they claim to see, but only at the strategic nuclear level, where there is still a rough equivalence between the forces of the two sides, are they really taken seriously. Local and limited clashes here or there are still conceivable, but it is not possible to write a convincing scenario for a full-scale continent-spanning conventional war in Europe today.

There are only two places on the planet where very large and up-to-date military forces still face each other in overtly hostile postures: India's borders with Pakistan and China, and the Korean peninsula. In both these cases, too, nuclear weapons are to hand. The Taiwan Strait between the People's Republic of China and Taiwan is a third potential candidate, but it's not there yet.

One must never forget the Middle East, but a military "solution" to the Arab-Israeli conflict is hard to imagine. In military terms Israel is the "dwarf superpower" of the region, and it has never lost a war against the Arabs. Moreover, as the Sunni Arab states, and in particular Saudi Arabia, grow ever more obsessed about the "threat" from Shia Iran, they are coming to view Israel as a potential ally rather than the perpetual enemy. Yet despite the region's well-earned reputation for frequent, futile, and often unwinnable wars, it's hard to believe in a major conventional war involving all the Shia-ruled countries (Iran, Iraq, and Syria, plus possibly Lebanon) versus all the Sunni Arab countries (Egypt, Saudi Arabia, the UAE, and the smaller Gulf states) plus Israel and maybe Turkey. It would be like herding cats.

Why does Israel win all its wars?

Israel has access to the latest generation of American weapons. It receives a huge annual subsidy to its defense budget from the United States.

Its population is more educated, more technologically proficient, and more accustomed to large, impersonal bureaucracies and hierarchies.

Thanks to its classic European mobilization system, Israel has put more troops on the battlefield than its much more populous Arab neighbors in four out of its five "conventional" wars.

It enjoys "interior lines" of communication: it can move troops from the Egyptian border to the Syrian, Jordanian, or Lebanese borders literally overnight.

Unlike most of the neighboring countries, Israel is a democratic and relatively equal society, at least for its Jewish citizens. This fosters a sense of unity, high morale, and resilience in adversity.

It has enjoyed a monopoly of nuclear weapons in the region for the past sixty years.

Most of today's small conventional wars have reassuringly little to offer military analysts in the way of new tactical and strategic lessons, but they do come along from time to time. In the Armenia-Azerbaijan war of 2020 Turkish-made missile-firing Bayraktar TB2 drones and Israeli-made "kamikaze" drones destroyed the majority of Armenian tanks, artillery, as well as multiple rocket-launch and surface-to-air missile systems, in just six weeks, by which time the Armenians had lost the war. A single new technology can sometimes have a decisive effect when it first appears in combat—but once both sides in a conflict have that new technology in adequate amounts and have absorbed the early tactical lessons on how it is best deployed and employed, the loss rates tend to equalize (if not necessarily decrease).

The world in the early twenth-first century presents an unfamiliar aspect. Cross-border wars between conventionally equipped armies, the staple of international politics down the ages, have virtually disappeared from the Americas, Oceania, and most of Asia. Measured against an admittedly terrible past, traditional "conventional" war actually seems to be declining—whereas it has been a golden age for guerrilla war and "terrorism."

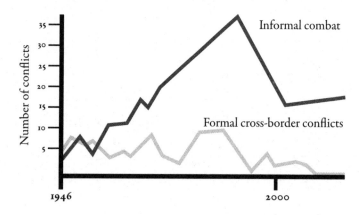

Everywhere and Nowhere

Guerrillas are not soldiers, and in modern times they generally do not serve a recognized state, but they certainly apply force for political ends: what they do is war, therefore, not random violence.

> Wherever we arrived, they disappeared; whenever we left, they arrived. They were everywhere and nowhere, they had no tangible center which could be attacked.
>
> French officer fighting Spanish guerrillas, 1810[5]

Guerrilla warfare as a form of resistance to foreign occupation gained prominence in the Napoleonic wars, when both the Spanish who gave the technique its name (*guerrilla* = "little war") and the Germans waged large guerrilla campaigns against French occupying forces. But it was not seen as a potentially decisive military technique even in World War II, when it was widely employed against German and Japanese occupation forces, mainly because it lacked a strategy for final victory.

So long as the guerrillas remained dispersed in the hills, forests, or swamps and indulged in only hit-and-run raiding, they could take a constant but limited toll on the army of the occupying power. They might also carry out what would today be called "terrorist" attacks in the cities—but they couldn't clear their enemies out of the urban centers of power without coming into the open. And if they ever did engage the occupying forces in open combat, the enemy's heavy weapons would smash them.

What changed after World War II was that the rural guerrilla technique spread into the European colonial empires. As in the occupied countries of Europe in 1939–45, guerrillas in the French, British, Dutch, and Portuguese colonies had no difficulty in mobilizing their fellow countrymen against the foreign occupiers. But as in the occupied countries of Europe, they had no way to win a decisive military victory against the well-equipped regular forces of the imperial power in question. It turned out, however, that the guerrillas didn't need a military victory. If they could make it very expensive for the colonial power to stay, and continue to do so indefinitely, then the colonial power would eventually decide to cut its losses and go home.

The pattern was repeated many times in the two decades after 1945, in Indonesia, Kenya, Algeria, Malaya, Cyprus, Vietnam, South Yemen, and many other places. In most cases, it was the guerrilla leaders themselves who inherited power: Sukarno in

Indonesia, Jomo Kenyatta in Kenya, the FLN in Algeria, and so on. Once the European imperial powers finally grasped their own fatal vulnerability to this technique, the decolonization process in many of their remaining colonies was completed without need for a guerrilla war.

WHEN GUERRILLA WAR WORKS

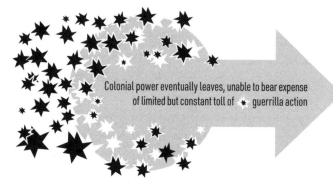

Colonial power eventually leaves, unable to bear expense of limited but constant toll of ✦ guerrilla action

At the time, the seemingly irresistible spread of rural guerrilla wars caused great alarm and despondency in the major Western powers, because most post-1945 guerrilla movements followed some version of the Marxist ideology preached by the West's international rival-in-chief, the Soviet Union. This led to a belief in the West that it was Soviet and/or Chinese expansionism, rather than resentment of foreign rule, that lay behind these guerrilla wars.

In fact, the Asian, African, and Arab revolutionary leaders of the 1950s and 1960s learned their Marxism in London and Paris, not in Moscow. The full-scale US military commitment to Vietnam in 1965 was not only made for the wrong reason—to thwart perceived Soviet expansionism acting through the Chinese—but at the wrong time. By 1965 the wave of guerrilla wars in the "Third World" was coming to its natural end: apart from Indochina, only southern Africa and South Yemen were still the scenes of active guerrilla campaigns against imperial rule. In order to win its Asian guerrilla war, the United States, driven by ideology, was willing to spend far more money and sacrifice many more lives (55,000) than the Europeans had been, but the equation worked for the Vietnamese as it had for everybody else: they just had to hang on long enough and not lose, and the American public would rebel against the cost and the casualties and give them a win. That happened in 1968, although the final American withdrawal was not until 1973.

Viet-Cong guerrillas crossing a river in 1966

The former Soviet Union was an autocracy with tight media controls, but by the 1980s it was equally vulnerable on the issue of casualties. Only fifteen thousand Soviet soldiers were killed during the country's ten-year military intervention in Afghanistan, but that produced Vietnam-like effects on Russian public opinion and forced Moscow to pull its troops out of Afghanistan in 1989. Indeed, Moscow's conduct of its post-2015 intervention in the Syrian civil war showed a reluctance to incur major military casualties just as intense as that in Washington.

The disappearance of the colonial/anti-imperial context in which the rural guerrilla technique originally flourished has drastically diminished its utility, because it hardly ever works against a locally based government supported by the most powerful local ethnic group. There is no foreign occupation to attract recruits to one's cause, and the endgame that delivered victory in anti-colonial struggles no longer applies. A locally based government cannot cut its losses and "go home" if the cost of fighting a counter-insurgency campaign gets too high. Where would it go? The exceptional cases of Eritrea and South Sudan prove the rule: in most of the newly independent countries, separatist groups fighting for independence cannot wear down the will of a locally based government and army.

WHEN GUERRILLA WAR DOESN'T WORK

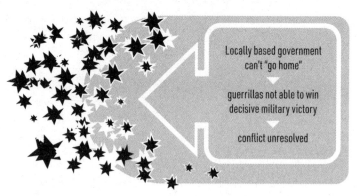

Locally based government
can't "go home"

guerrillas not able to win
decisive military victory

conflict unresolved

The one great exception to all these rules was the fifteen-year rural guerrilla war, eventually growing into a full-scale conventional war, in which the Chinese Communist Party finally seized power from the equally Chinese Kuomintang Party in 1949.

> In every battle, concentrate an absolutely superior force, encircle the enemy forces completely, strive to wipe them out thoroughly and do not let any escape from the net.
>
> Mao Zedong, 1947[6]

Mao would never have given that order in the 1930s or the early 1940s, when he was waging a classic guerrilla campaign against the Japanese invaders of China and the Chinese Communist Party's domestic enemy, the ruling Kuomintang (KMT). Instead, he followed the standard rules of guerrilla warfare: ambush small groups of the enemy, but never stand and fight against their main forces. By 1947, however, the Japanese had surrendered and the KMT were reeling. In just two years the People's Liberation Army grew fourfold to two million men and came out into the open to beat the corrupt, divided, and incompetent KMT government in a series of stand-up battles.

Mao Zedong during the 1930s

Mao achieved the Holy Grail of guerrilla war. With no support from outside and no anti-foreign resentment to help him, he turned his guerrilla soldiers into a real army and beat the existing Chinese government in open battle. It was a brilliant accomplishment, and many other revolutionary groups tried to follow his example. Only two succeeded: Fidel Castro's little band of brothers who came down from the Sierra Maestre in 1959, and the Sandinistas in Nicaragua in 1979. In both cases, the circumstances were very different than China's under the Kuomintang. The enemies faced by

Castro's 26th of July Movement and the Sandinistas were governments so extraordinarily wicked and incompetent that they made even the KMT look good, and both movements could hold the patriotic high ground by exploiting the anti-American sentiment that ran strongly in those countries after so much US intervention.

And that's it. There are still rural guerrilla movements hanging on in the more rugged parts of some Third World countries, but they have little hope of success against local governments that can credibly invoke nationalism on their own side. If they ever try to move up from assassinations, car-bombs, and hit-and-run raids to more ambitious operations involving large units that will stand and fight, they simply give the government's army the targets it had been hoping for. By the 1970s it had become clear that rural guerrilla warfare was no longer a promising revolutionary technique.

"Urban Guerrilla Warfare"

This realization drove numbers of disappointed Latin American revolutionaries into random terrorism (or rather, "urban guerrilla warfare," as it came to be known). The initial goal of the Latin American originators of this doctrine, notably the Montoneros of Argentina, the Tupamaros of Uruguay, and Brazilian revolutionaries like Carlos Marighella, was to drive the target regimes into extreme repression. It was what French Marxists called "*la politique du pire*" (the strategy of making things worse).

By assassinations, bank robberies, kidnappings, hijacking, and the like, calculated to inflict maximum embarrassment on the government, the urban guerrillas aimed to provoke the overthrow of democratic governments by tough military regimes, or to drive existing military regimes into even stricter and more unpopular security measures. If the regime resorted to counterterror, torture, "disappearances," and death squads, so much the better, for the goal was to alienate the population from the government.

> It is necessary to turn political crisis into armed conflict by performing violent actions that will force those in power to transform the political situation of the country into a military situation. That will alienate the masses, who, from then on, will revolt against the army and the police and blame them for this state of things.
> Carlos Marighella, *Mini-Manual of the Urban Guerrilla*[7]

Alas, urban guerrilla war had the same fatal flaw as rural guerrilla warfare outside the late-colonial environment: it lacked a good endgame. The theory said that when the guerrillas had succeeded in summoning up a brutally repressive regime, the populace would then rise up and destroy its oppressors. But just how was it to accomplish this feat? Armed urban uprisings have rarely succeeded since the nineteenth century.

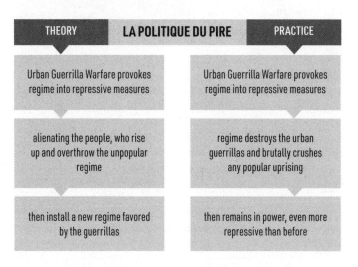

THEORY	LA POLITIQUE DU PIRE	PRACTICE
Urban Guerrilla Warfare provokes regime into repressive measures		Urban Guerrilla Warfare provokes regime into repressive measures
alienating the people, who rise up and overthrow the unpopular regime		regime destroys the urban guerrillas and brutally crushes any popular uprising
then install a new regime favored by the guerrillas		then remains in power, even more repressive than before

In various Latin American countries, the urban guerrillas accomplished step one of their strategy: the creation of thoroughly nasty military regimes dedicated to destroying them. But these governments then proceeded to do precisely that. In every Latin American country where *la politique du pire* was attempted, most urban guerrillas ended up dead or in exile.

The faint and even more foolish echoes of these Latin American terrorist strategies were the profoundly unserious terrorist movements that flourished in western Europe and North America during the 1970s and 1980s. Their main ideological guru was the American academic Herbert Marcuse, who wrote of the need to "unmask the repressive tolerance of the liberal bourgeoisie" through acts of creative violence that would force them to drop their liberal disguises and reveal their true repressive nature. This was designer terrorism, as much about "attitude" as about real politics, and although it killed several hundred people and generated several hundred thousand headlines, it never threatened any government anywhere. Leonard Cohen captured the naiveté and narcissism of the developed world's urban guerrillas in his sardonic song "First We Take Manhattan."

The Baader Meinhof Complex film poster

> *I'm guided by a signal in the heavens.*
> *I'm guided by this birth-mark on my skin.*
> *I'm guided by the beauty of our weapons.*
> *First we take Manhattan. Then we take Berlin.*

If the Baader-Meinhof Gang in Germany, the Red Brigades in Italy, the Symbionese Liberation Army, the Weathermen in the US, the Japanese Red Army, and all the rest had any influence whatever on events, it was chiefly as bogeymen useful to right-wing governments seeking to vilify their legitimate left-wing opponents. Nationalist urban guerrillas operating from a religious or ethnic minority base like the Provisional Irish Republican Army (IRA) in Northern Ireland and Euskadi ta Askatasuna (ETA) in Spain's Basque provinces showed greater staying power, but both have now made peace with the governments they fought.

Two terrorist groups did find a way to make an impact on events, however. Both made their mark with international operations; both had political aims that did not require the overthrow of the target governments; and both were Arab.

Palestine

The Palestine Liberation Organization (PLO) was founded by Yasser Arafat in 1964 to coordinate a strategy for the armed groups forming in the refugee camps where large numbers of Palestinians lived. Arafat's key insight was to realize that while these groups stood no chance of defeating Israel and regaining their homes by direct attacks, their energies might produce results if applied to a different goal.

Arafat and his colleagues understood the importance of rebranding the "refugees" as "Palestinians." So long as they were seen by non-Arabs (and even by some Arabs) as merely generic "Arab refugees," they could theoretically be resettled anywhere in the Arab world. Their only hope of ever going home was to convince the world that there was such an identity as "Palestinian," for to call people by that name is implicitly to accept that they have a legitimate claim to the land of Palestine.

What kind of campaign might convince the world that there really are Palestinians? Not an ordinary advertising campaign, certainly, but if you carry out shocking acts of violence, then the media have to report them—and in order to explain them, they will have to talk about Palestinians. In September 1970, PLO "guerrillas" simultaneously hijacked four airliners, flew them to a desert airfield in Jordan, and destroyed them before the world's television cameras after the passengers had been removed. Subsequent PLO attacks cost many lives, but this was international terrorism with a rational and achievable objective: not to bring Israel to its knees, but to force the world to accept the existence of a Palestinian people who must be active participants in the discussion of their own fate.

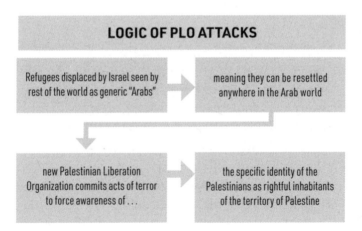

LOGIC OF PLO ATTACKS

Refugees displaced by Israel seen by rest of the world as generic "Arabs"

meaning they can be resettled anywhere in the Arab world

new Palestinian Liberation Organization commits acts of terror to force awareness of . . .

the specific identity of the Palestinians as rightful inhabitants of the territory of Palestine

Once that objective was achieved in the late 1980s, the PLO called off the terrorists (though some maverick splinter groups who didn't understand the strategy continued to make pointless terror attacks on their own). For the next decade the PLO pursued the goal of a negotiated peace with Israel, with the high point being the signing of the Oslo Accords in Washington in 1993. However, Arafat and his key negotiating partner, the Israeli Prime Minister Yitzhak Rabin, both found their freedom of action increasingly limited by "rejectionist" forces in their own camps who refused to accept the kinds of concessions on territory and on the right of return for refugees that were necessary for a peace settlement.

After Rabin was assassinated by a right-wing Jewish extremist in 1995, Palestinian terrorist attacks resumed, this time in Israel itself in the midst of an election campaign. The authors of these attacks were not the PLO, but the rising Islamist movements who rejected any deal that would see a Palestinian state created in just a small part of the former British mandate of Palestine. Here was another terrorist operation with a rational and achievable goal—the goal this time being to thwart Arafat's "two-state" strategy.

The bombing campaign of Hamas and Islamic Jihad, which particularly targeted buses to produce high Jewish casualties, was intended to drive Israeli voters away from Rabin's successor Shimon Peres, expected to win easily on a sympathy vote after Rabin's assassination, and into the arms of Binyamin Netanyahu, a closet rejectionist who could be counted on to stall indefinitely on peace negotiations. It worked, and there was virtually no progress on a peace settlement for the next three years. Nor indeed since: the rejectionists on both sides are "objective allies," as the Marxists would describe them, whose shared purpose is to stymie the two-state solution, and they have been successful.

Hijacked plane strikes the World Trade Center, September 11, 2001

The Islamist project animating al-Qaeda, Islamic State, and their various clones and affiliates starts from the proposition that the current sorry plight of the Muslim countries is due to the fact that they are half-Westernized and lax in their observance of Islam. This situation will only change when Muslims are living their faith as God truly intends it to be lived—or rather, according to the Islamists' somewhat extreme interpretation of what God's intentions might be.

Upon this foundation a two-stage project for changing the world is built. In stage one, all existing governments of Muslim countries must be overthrown so that the Islamists can take their places and use the power of the state to bring Muslims back to the right ways of believing and behaving. Then God will help them to unite the whole of the Muslim world in a single, borderless superstate that will take on and overthrow the domination of the West. In the more extreme formulations, this will culminate with the conversion of the entire world to Islam.

Relatively few Muslims accept this Islamist analysis, let alone support the project, but their numbers are greater in the Arab world than elsewhere because it is in these countries that rage and despair at the current situation are strongest. As a result, Islamist revolutionary groups have been active in most of the larger Arab states for at least three decades. To achieve their first goal of overthrowing existing governments and taking power themselves, they frequently resorted to terrorism. Not surprisingly, they failed to win power anywhere. Terrorism didn't work for the Tupamaros, it didn't work for the Baader-Meinhof Gang, and there is no reason that it should work for the Islamists either.

What *can* overthrow a government (apart from a military coup, which is an unlikely way for Islamists to come to power) is a million people in the street—but first you have to get the million people out, and for Islamists they just haven't come. The mass of people simply don't like or trust the Islamists enough to risk their own lives to bring them to power. The result in some countries has been a bloody stalemate between Islamists and governments, with most people sitting out the struggle and wishing a curse on both their houses. This deadlock was already well established when Osama bin Laden founded al-Qaeda in Afghanistan at the beginning of the 1990s.

> The nations of infidels have all united against Muslims . . . This is a new battle, a great battle, similar to the great battles of Islam like the conquest of Jerusalem . . . [The Americans] come out to fight Islam in the name of fighting terrorism.
>
> Osama bin Laden, October 2002

Al-Qaeda's strategy was not to attack Arab governments, but to go directly after the West. Yet we must assume that the real goal of al-Qaeda and its various Islamist rivals and successors is still to bring about revolutions that will raise Islamists to power in Arab and other Muslim countries, and so begin the reformation of the people in the true path of Islamic observance. How would attacking the West directly help to bring those revolutions any nearer?

Terrorists never advertise their real strategies, but almost certainly al-Qaeda's was the *politique du pire* all over again, this time in an international context. Only a fool would believe that a terrorist attack on the United States, causing three thousand deaths, would make the US government abandon its client governments in the Muslim world. Any sensible person would know that Washington's reaction would be one or more large, armed incursions into the Muslim world in an attempt to stamp out the roots of the terrorism.

Bin Laden and his associates were neither ignorant nor stupid. Their real strategy was to sucker the United States into marching into the Muslim world in big army boots, trusting that America's actions would drive a great many Muslims into the arms of their local Islamist organizations. Then the longed-for revolts against pro-Western governments might finally come to pass and bring the Islamists to power.

If that was the strategic purpose of al-Qaeda's 9/11 attacks on New York and Washington, it has to be admitted that bin Laden had a reasonable return on his investment: within twenty months, the United States had invaded and occupied two Muslim countries containing fifty million people. The images accompanying the invasions caused great distress and humiliation to Muslims, especially in the Arab world, and the inevitable brutalities and mistakes of the subsequent military occupations of Afghanistan and Iraq produced a steady flow of further images in the same vein.

The anger these caused did push millions of Muslims, especially in the Arab world, into the arms of Islamist revolutionary organizations, but the long-term consequences in the Middle East have not been revolutionary. In Afghanistan, indeed, the immediate result of the US invasion in 2001 was the overthrow of the sole existing Islamist government in the Muslim world, the Taliban.

It took twenty years for the Taliban to drive the Americans and their allies out again, but now that the status quo ante has been restored, the Taliban are likely to take no more interest in global jihad than they did before the American invasion. Their focus has always been exclusively domestic.

The US attack on Saddam Hussein's regime in Iraq must have come as a surprise to bin Laden, since the Iraqi dictator did not cooperate with Islamist revolutionaries; he killed them. The American invasion did, however, generate an Islamist resistance movement among Sunni Iraqis of the sort that bin Laden was hoping to stimulate, led by al-Qaeda, that killed about 4,500 American soldiers in ten years. In 2014 it morphed into the ephemeral "Islamic State of Iraq and Syria" (ISIS), which ruled over between eight and twelve million people in parts of those two countries. By 2019, however, "Islamic State" was defeated and largely expunged, although al-Qaeda continues to operate as a guerrilla and terrorist organization in various parts of the Middle East and Africa.

Could the United States have done it differently? Not invading Iraq would certainly have helped, but popular anger in the United States after 9/11 made it very hard for the Bush administration to avoid invading Afghanistan—just as the al-Qaeda leader intended.

An additional factor in enabling the invasion was the US military's obsession with "bases." Such facilities are indispensable for regular armies but are actually irrelevant for revolutionaries using a terrorist strategy. The al-Qaeda camp in

Afghanistan was a handy place to indoctrinate volunteers, but it was a dispensable luxury: the planning for 9/11 was mainly done in Germany, and the pilots were trained in the United States. Organizations like al-Qaeda are decentralized civilian networks with minimal logistic requirements, and the right tools to deal with them are normally police forces, intelligence-gathering, and security measures, not an army.

Even now, after twenty years of missed learning opportunities, the military obsession with a revived "terrorist base" in Afghanistan persists, but the real terrorists will remain dispersed and almost invisible. Their ability to do harm will wax and wane, but they are unlikely to go out of business entirely. So how big might the "international terrorist threat" get?

Thus far, al-Qaeda and its various Islamist rivals are still operating in the same technological universe that the PLO exploited fifty years ago (although with radically different political objectives). It discovered a new use for hijacked airliners by training suicide bombers to become pilots, but there do not appear to be many undiscovered techniques of similar power lying around waiting to be tried. Down to the time of writing, all of al-Qaeda's subsequent attacks have been thoroughly conventional low-tech bombings and mass shootings causing at the most a couple of hundred deaths and more often only a few. The increasingly common "lone wolf" attacks, carried out by individuals whose only contact with al-Qaeda and its ilk is through visiting their websites, make detection more difficult but also tend to produce lower casualties.

What strategic purpose do these attacks serve, now that it has been demonstrated that even major Western invasions of Muslim countries do not drive sufficient numbers of Muslims into the arms of the Islamist revolutionaries? None comes to mind: these activities, although they once had a coherent strategic rationale, are now futile and pointless. Why do Islamist activists go on doing it? Because of devotion to the ideology or hatred of the infidel; because it gives meaning to their lives; because they can't think what else to do. Islamist terrorism will no doubt continue long past its sell-by date, but generational turnover may dispose of it in the end.

Even terrorism with so-called weapons of mass destruction does not rise to the level of an existential threat. The Japanese sect Aum Shinrikyo managed to release a sarin-type nerve gas on the Tokyo subway in 1995; only twelve people were killed. The practical problem with both chemical and biological agents is dispersal; the terrorists would get better results for less effort with nail bombs.

A nuclear weapon in terrorist hands would be a far bigger problem, but a single nuclear explosion would be a local disaster comparable in scale to the Krakatoa volcanic explosion of 1883 or the Tokyo earthquake of 1923. We should obviously strive to prevent it, but even a nuclear detonation in some unfortunate city some time in the future would in all likelihood not stampede the world into doing what the terrorists want—and what they almost always want is an overreaction. Terrorism is a kind of political jiujitsu in which small, weak groups use the modest amounts of force at their disposal to trick their far more powerful opponents—usually states—into responding in ways that harm the opponent's cause and serve the terrorists' own purposes.

The world lived for forty years with the daily threat of a global nuclear holocaust that could destroy hundreds of cities and hundreds of millions of lives at a stroke. It can live with the distant possibility that a terrorist group might one day get possession of a single nuclear weapon and bring horror to a single city. The point is not to panic, and not to lose patience.

I'm afraid that terrorism didn't begin on 9/11 and it will be around for a long time. I was very surprised by the announcement of a war on terrorism because terrorism has been around for thirty-five years . . . [and it] will be around while there are people with grievances. There are things we can do to improve the situation, but there will always be terrorism. One can be misled by talking about a war, as though in some way you can defeat it.

Stella Rimington, former Director General of MI5,
September 2002[8]

CHAPTER 10

The End of War

The Way Back

> The good news for humans is that it looks like peaceful conditions, once established, can be maintained. And if baboons can do it, why not us?
>
> Frans de Waal, Yerkes Primate Center, Emory University

About thirty years ago, a disaster struck the Forest Troop of baboons in Kenya. The toughest males in the troop would regularly forage in the garbage dump at a nearby tourist resort. One day, they all ate meat that was infected with bovine tuberculosis and promptly died, leaving behind only the less aggressive males—who avoided the dump because there were regular fights there with another baboon band. And the Forest Troop's whole culture changed.

The baboon and the neuroscientist, Robert Sapolsky

When neuroscientist Robert Sapolsky first studied the Forest Troop in 1979–82, it was a typical, utterly vicious baboon society. Male baboons are normally so obsessed with status that they are permanently on a hair trigger for aggression— and this isn't just directed at male rivals of equal status. Lower-ranking males are routinely bullied and terrorized, and even females (who weigh half as much as males) are frequently attacked. But after the mass die-off of the bullies, the surviving members relaxed and began treating one another more decently.

The males still fight with other males of equal rank, but they don't beat up social inferiors, and they don't attack the females at all. Everybody spends much more time on grooming, huddling close together, and other friendly social behavior, and stress levels even for the lowest-ranking individuals (as measured by hormone samples) are far lower than in other baboon troops. Most important of all, these new behaviors have become entrenched in the troop's culture.

Male baboons rarely live more than eighteen years, so the low-status survivors of the original disaster are all gone now. And since male baboons must leave their birth troop and join a different one, the range of male personalities in Forest Troop must have returned to the normal distribution, from dominance-oriented alphas to timid and submissive losers who would never normally stand a chance. Yet the behavior of the troop has not returned to baboon-normal: levels of aggressiveness remain comparatively low and random attacks on social inferiors and females are rare.[1]

We primates are very malleable and adaptive in our cultures; even baboons are not shackled by their genes to the viciously aggressive norms of baboon society. Human beings today live quite comfortably in pseudo-bands called nations that can be over ten million times bigger than the bands our ancestors lived in until the rise of civilization. We went from monkey-king tyranny to equality in our hunter-gatherer days, then back to steep, militarized hierarchies as civilization evolved, and have now returned to a heavily modified form of egalitarianism. Given the right incentives, weaning ourselves away from war ought not to be impossible. And we have certainly been given the right incentives.

Holiday from History

> You can say more truly of the First World War than of the Second or of the Third that if the people had known what was going to happen, they wouldn't have done it. The Second World War—they knew more, and they accepted it. And the Third World War—alas, in a sense they know everything about it, they know what will happen, and they do nothing. I don't know the answer.
>
> A. J. P. Taylor, author of *The Origins of the Second World War*

When Alan Taylor talked like that in 1982, it resonated strongly with a generation that had spent its life waiting for World War III to happen. Then the collapse of the Soviet Union and the end of the Cold War convinced most people that World War III wasn't ever going to happen, as if there were no systemic causes and the only reason for it ever to have happened was the wicked Soviets. There followed a full generation when all that most people worried about was outbreaks of ethnic cleansing and the occasional terrorist attack. The little wars that still occurred didn't really threaten the developed countries and could be dealt with or not as the moral mood of the moment dictated. Now, however, the fear of nuclear war is back, at least for a visit, and a new generation is learning the vocabulary of deterrence strategy. But by and large it's still only the people who work within or study the international system—diplomats and professional soldiers, some statesmen, and a few historians—who understand that it was the structure of the system itself that produced the cycle of great-power conflicts we now call world wars.

We haven't entirely wasted the relatively peaceful time we were given after the end of the Cold War. The US-led United Nations campaign to expel the Iraqi invaders from occupied Kuwait in 1991 was the first time UN rules against aggression had been enforced by military action since the Korean War forty years before. The UN rules protecting the sovereignty of independent states were bent several times in the 1990s so that international military interventions could prevent genocides (although the worst case, in Rwanda/eastern Congo, was ignored). But little was done to increase the authority of the Security Council or to entrench the habit of multilateralism, for the unilateralist current was already running strongly in the United States, by this time the sole global superpower.

A certain amount of hubris was to be expected after the United States' apparent triumph in the Cold War; even before it, the glorification of national military power was part of the political culture in Washington. In 2001 hubris and militarism fused in a project for American hegemony commonly called *Pax Americana*, whose neoconservative proponents ended up controlling US military and foreign policy under President George W. Bush. The Bush administration launched a sustained assault on multilateral institutions: it abandoned the Anti-Ballistic Missile Treaty, tried to sabotage the International Criminal Court, rejected amendments to make the conventions against chemical and biological weapons more enforceable, and used the terrorist attacks of September 11, 2001, as the pretext for an invasion of Iraq in 2003, which also constituted a deliberate attack on the authority of the Security Council.

By the end of Bush's second term in 2008, any progress during the 1990s, particularly with regard to trust among the great powers, had been lost. The advent of the Trump presidency in 2017 brought a fresh American assault on multilateral institutions, and while President Biden is clearly an improvement, the "Washington consensus" on foreign policy that Biden once incarnated is not well suited to the future that likely awaits us. The holiday from history may be almost over.

Three Great Changes

Three great changes are underway that could tip the international system back into the old disorder: global heating, the rise of new great powers, and nuclear proliferation. The ramshackle system we have designed to keep the peace will be under acute stress.

Rising global temperature will have disastrous effects on food production in the tropics and subtropics at least a generation before similar impacts are felt in the rich countries of the temperate latitudes. The consequence will be famines in those countries nearer to the equator and millions-strong waves of desperate refugees trying to get into the developed countries. The borders will slam shut, of course, but the only way to keep them shut against such numbers may be some "exemplary" killing of those who try to breach them. The net result is likely to be a widespread breakdown in international cooperation (including cooperation in dealing with climate change), as it is difficult for countries to make agreements and compromises when one country is killing another's citizens.

At the same time, the international system will be trying to adjust to the rise of new great powers and the relative decline of most of the existing powers. The ticket to superpower status in the world of 2040 will be brutally simple: only countries of subcontinental scale with populations near to or over half a billion people. Only three candidates will qualify: the US, China, and India.

India, which has no credible prospect of overtaking either of the other two candidates in the next generation, has done the obvious thing and concluded an alliance of sorts with the

United States. India has already had one border war with China (in 1962), and "the enemy of my enemy is my friend."

China was the undisputed superpower in the parts of the world known to the Chinese for most of its history, and many Chinese feel a certain resentment that it has lost that status in the past three centuries. They therefore believe that in a just world it should recover that position—and if justice does not spontaneously deliver that result, perhaps it needs a little help.

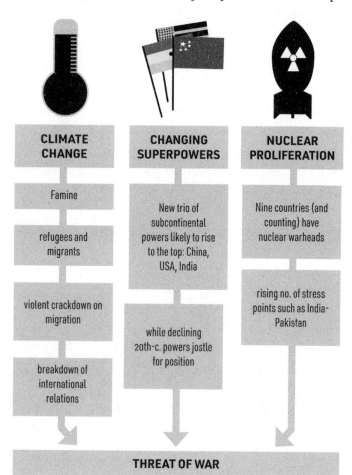

CLIMATE CHANGE

Famine

refugees and migrants

violent crackdown on migration

breakdown of international relations

CHANGING SUPERPOWERS

New trio of subcontinental powers likely to rise to the top: China, USA, India

while declining 20th-c. powers jostle for position

NUCLEAR PROLIFERATION

Nine countries (and counting) have nuclear warheads

rising no. of stress points such as India-Pakistan

THREAT OF WAR

However, China is not a classic expansionist power like sixteenth-century Spain or early twentieth-century Japan. None of its territorial claims extend beyond areas that it once dominated, nor are they so important to China's interests that it would fight to the death for them. Nevertheless, its growing military power and its often belligerent rhetoric do make the neighbors nervous, and we know where this sort of thing usually ended up in the past.

On the other hand, China may never overtake the United States, because its economic growth has slowed drastically in the past decade and its population is about to go into a steep decline. The current Chinese regime will never relinquish its claim to Taiwan (nor would any successor, in all likelihood), but the current balance of forces does not encourage adventurism in Beijing.

Like the last great-power confrontation, the Cold War, this one may turn out to be manageable, and eventually end peacefully. In the past, war was the normal way the international system adjusted to accommodate the demands of rising powers at the expense of those declining, but nobody wants to go through that again with twenty-first-century weapons.

Lastly, nuclear weapons are spreading. Between 1945 and 1964, the "Permanent Five" great powers on the UN Security Council—the United States, the Soviet Union, Britain, France, and China—all tested their first nuclear weapons, and one other country, Israel, secretly developed them without openly testing them. There was then a lengthy delay before other nuclear powers emerged.

At various points in the late 1970s or 1980s, Argentina, Brazil, South Africa, Iraq, Iran, and North Korea embarked on nuclear weapons projects, but only one, North Korea's, resulted in an actual nuclear deterrent force. Since the North Koreans clearly understand the concept of deterrence, and in particular that the ability to deliver one or two nuclear weapons on US cities is enough to protect them from American attack, their force will probably stay small and may eventually be accepted by Washington as nonthreatening. India and Pakistan, unfortunately, are in a different situation.

North Korean submarine-launched ballistic missile showcased in Pyongyang, April 15, 2017

India tested its first "peaceful nuclear explosive" in 1974, ostensibly for civil engineering projects, but really to create a deterrent against Chinese nuclear weapons (the two countries had fought a brief border war in 1962). Meanwhile Pakistan, having fought and lost three wars with India in the previous quarter century, felt obliged to keep up and embarked on its own secret nuclear program. That rivalry culminated in 1998 with first India, then Pakistan, publicly testing half a dozen nuclear weapons. The two countries are now in the *use 'em or lose 'em* phase of a nuclear arms race (also known as "launch on warning"), where the relatively unprotected weapons of both sides (around 150 nuclear warheads each) are vulnerable to a surprise first strike that would destroy the great majority of them. Moreover, their warning time of an incoming strike might be as little as four minutes, not the fifteen minutes-plus that the Americans and the Soviets had at the height of the Cold War. If the two countries were already in a shooting war (as they have been three times in the past half century), and the screens lit up with incoming missile trajectories, that's not much time to decide whether the tracks are real. An all-out nuclear exchange would be bad enough for India and Pakistan, but if a large proportion of those weapons were used on cities, creating perhaps a hundred simultaneous firestorms, we might all find ourselves on the threshold of a global nuclear winter.

> There will be consequences to [India's decision in Aug. 2019 to strip Kashmir of its special status] . . . If a conventional war starts, anything could happen. We will fight, and when a nuclear-armed country fights to the end it will have consequences far beyond the borders. It will have consequences for the world.
> Pakistan's prime minister Imran Khan to the UN General Assembly, September 27, 2019[2]

The world's record on nuclear proliferation over the past forty years is not that bad: only three more countries, making a total of nine. The "firebreak" that we began building against actual nuclear weapon use after Hiroshima in 1945 has held for three quarters of a century. But getting through the rest of this century without the first-magnitude catastrophe of a global nuclear war will require good management and good luck.

Cooperate or Else

There is no point dreaming that we can leap straight into some neverland of world government and universal brotherhood. We will have to solve the problem of war within the context of the existing state system. In practice, that means preserving and extending the multilateral system we have been building (with many interruptions and failures) since the end of World War II. The rising powers must be absorbed into a system that emphasizes cooperation and makes room for them, rather than one that deals in confrontation and raw military power.

This is exactly what we have been trying to do for several generations, of course, with very limited success. But in all that time nobody has come up with a more plausible idea, which suggests there is no easier path.

The state of international anarchy that compelled every nation to arm itself for war had such an obvious remedy that it arose almost spontaneously after the first total war in 1918. What was required was clearly a pooling of sovereignty, at least in matters concerning war and peace, by all the states of the world; and the victors of World War I promptly created the League of Nations. But the devil is in the details: the idea that the nations of the world will band together to deter or punish aggression by some maverick country is fine in principle, but who defines the aggressor, and who pays the money and the lives needed to make him stop?

Every member of the League of Nations also knew that if the organization ever gained real authority, it could end up being used against them, so no major government was willing to let it have any real power. They got World War II, a war so costly in both lives and money that the victors made a second attempt in 1945 to create an international organization truly capable of preventing war. The winners of World War II were frightened people. When they sat down to negotiate the Charter of the United Nations in San Francisco in 1945, they actually made war illegal. The new UN Charter forbade the use of force against another country except in strict self-defense or in obedience to the Security Council's orders—and those orders would be issued only in order to stop some country from attacking another UN member. So there it was: from the bad old days to a new world of law where war was banned in a single breathtaking leap.

Not really. Everybody understood that the creation of the United Nations was the launch of a hundred-year project. The survivors of the worst war in history weren't the least bit naive about what they were trying to do. Proof of that is the brutal realism they brought to the rules for enforcement.

Normal international treaties pretend that all sovereign states are equal. Not the UN Charter: it gave the five victorious great powers of 1945—the United States, the United Kingdom, France, the Soviet Union, and China—permanent seats on the Security Council, while other countries must rotate through on two-year terms. To order military action against a country accused of aggression, the great powers must convince enough temporary members to win a majority vote in the fifteen-member Security Council, but any one of the great powers can veto action, even if the majority in favor is fourteen to one. The people who wrote the rules frankly acknowledged that the great powers were more equal than the others. And that's because they were serious about getting the new system to work.

Persuading the great powers to sign up to these rules was tricky. They were being asked to give up a tool—military power—that often let them get their way in the world. They knew that one day they, too, could be destroyed in a great-power war, so changing the international rules was in their own long-term self-interest, but they were being asked to give up a bird in the hand for one in the bush. The veto was what got them over this hurdle: it meant the UN could never take action against any of the great powers, and in effect it exempted them from the new international law. Other countries, though, had to obey it. If the Security Council agreed that their actions represented a danger to peace, they could face an international army operating under the UN flag. It happened to North Korea in 1950, and to Iraq in 1990.

The great powers were also expected to obey the law, and might face heavy pressure of various sorts if they didn't, but they could not be brought to book militarily. They could simply veto any Security Council resolution that condemned them. (As of March 2022, Russia/USSR had used its veto 120 times, United States 82 times, UK 29 times, France 16 times, and China 16 times.)

Russian Ambassador to the UN votes against US resolution to investigate alleged use of chemical weapons in Syria, April 10, 2018

In spite of all that pragmatism, it still didn't work. Within a few years the five permanent members of the Security Council had divided into two hostile military blocs, as victorious nations often do after a great war. It would have been a big historical surprise if they hadn't.

War Crimes

Another major innovation after World War II was "war crimes" trials. It was "victors' justice," to be sure: some of the laws under which senior German and Japanese officials and officers were charged had not existed when the alleged crimes were committed, but it was a bold and partly successful attempt to define and enforce proper behavior even amidst the cruelty and chaos of war. Miraculously, it turned out that no war crimes were committed by commanders on the winning side.

> At a certain place, I'm in battle. I have a unit that is advancing. I have a tank knocked out by the Germans. The four men inside get out, not wounded but stunned. Instead of coming back toward my lines, they head off toward the German line. The Germans, there—b–r–r—they killed them, right there. Some of my men see that and say: "They killed them without giving them a chance. That's wrong."
>
> Major Jacques Dextrase, Fusiliers Mont-Royal

Jacques Dextrase was a twenty-four-year-old major commanding a French-Canadian infantry company in Normandy in August 1944 when this incident occurred.

> OK. The battle continues and we take some prisoners. I pick someone to take the prisoners to the rear. When the man in charge of the prisoners comes to a bridge—he had made them run almost three miles—he says: "No, you lot blew up the bridges, you are going to swim." Well, you can well imagine that a man who has run three miles and then tries to swim . . . most of them drowned.
>
> And me, passing near there in my jeep, when I see thirty, forty, fifty bodies of drowned men . . . I wonder what

Dextrase was a good soldier who ended up as a full general and chief of defense staff of the Canadian Armed Forces. Canadians fought in every twentieth-century war of the West except Vietnam, and in that period lost almost twice as many military dead per capita as the United States. Yet although some war crimes had been codified in the Hague Conventions of 1899 and 1907, as late as 1944 Dextrase had nowhere to turn, in practice, when he discovered a war crime in his regiment. Administrative punishment and cover-up was the best he could do.

The Nuremberg principles of 1947 and the Geneva Conventions of 1949 changed that, and since then there has been a dramatic increase in the number of prosecutions for war crimes. Most Western armed forces remind their members at least annually of their legal obligations in wartime. So when the Australian army discovered war crimes had been committed by its troops in Afghanistan, its response was radically different.

Australian troops were in Afghanistan almost continuously from 2001 to 2021 as part of the US-led coalition supporting the US-installed government there against the Taliban and other Islamist insurgent forces. When rumours about the conduct of Australia's elite Special Air Services troops reached Special Operations Commander Jeff Sengelman, he commissioned military sociologist Dr. Samantha Crompfoets, a civilian, to look into the culture of the special forces. On the evidence of the interviews she carried out (one of which is quoted above) in 2016 the Inspector-General of the Australian Defense Force created an independent inquiry headed by Major-General Justice Paul Brereton, a reserve officer and a judge on the New South Wales Court of Appeal, to carry out a formal investigation.

Brereton's heavily redacted report, delivered in November 2020, found credible evidence for the murder of thirty-nine Afghans—prisoners of war, farmers, and other civilians—by twenty-five named Australian SAS soldiers in 2007–13. None of the killings took place in the heat of battle, the report said, and all occurred in circumstances that would, if accepted by a jury, constitute the war crime of murder. Most were the consequences of a "warrior culture" in which junior soldiers would be "blooded" (i.e., get their first kill) by shooting a prisoner on the orders of their patrol commander, typically a senior NCO. "Throw-downs" (captured weapons and radios) would then be placed by the victims' bodies and photographed to create a "cover story" for the purposes of operational reporting. And in the "Fat Lady's Arms," an unofficial bar that was set up inside the SAS base in Uruzgan province, soldiers would drink out of a hollow prosthetic leg that had been taken from the body of a dead Taliban fighter.

In a nationally televised response to the Brereton report, General Angus Campbell, the Chief of the Defense Force, accepted all 143 of Brereton's recommendations, referred the report to the Australian federal police for criminal investigation, apologized to the people of Afghanistan, condemned the "shameful" and "toxic" culture that had been allowed to flourish within the SAS, and supported calls to make helmet or body cameras compulsory for special forces on future deployments. It wasn't a perfect performance—he was a bit vague about how high up the chain of command the blame would be laid—but it was pretty good.

Inevitably there was a nationalist backlash. Campbell sought to strip the entire Special Operations Task Group of its "meritorious unit citation," which allowed those who wanted to shift public attention away from the war criminals to focus instead on the hurt allegedly felt by the three thousand other Australians who had served in the same unit in 2007–13. Campbell must have known this was coming; he just did it anyway.

The gulf between Dextrase's response and Campbell's is not a matter of personality or nationality; it is a question of dates. There has been a gradual transformation in the willingness of armies to hold their own members accountable for criminal behavior despite the moral complexity of the combat environment, and it does stem from the post-Second World War clarification and amplification of the laws of war. Little by little . . .

A Very Long Time

> It's going to be a very long time before governments are prepared in fact to submit to limitations on their national policies by an international body—not least because you've got a tremendous domestic opposition to it, very often.
>
> > Brian Urquhart, former under secretary-general,
> > United Nations

That "tremendous domestic opposition" is currently embodied in the populist/nationalist governments that were elected in various democratic countries (US, UK, Brazil, Poland,

Hungary, India, the Philippines), but the arch-populist Donald Trump has already lost office and this is no more the "end of history" than the nonviolent, anti-Communist revolutions of 1989 were. There is now a single global culture, with hundreds of local variants but still coherent enough to be swept by waves of political fashion, and the current fashion for populism is unlikely to be the last word. We might even look back and find ourselves grateful, at some future juncture, that this fashion had run its course before the going got really rough.

It isn't that the United Nations should have succeeded from the start but has instead failed. On the contrary: it was bound to be a relative failure, and that is no reason to despair. Progress will necessarily be measured in small steps even over decades. There is no point yearning for some universal Gandhi who can change the human heart and free us from our obsessions with national interest and power.

The reasons we behave as we do are not (just) stupid or paltry. We can never get all we want. This is why neighboring states have lived in a perpetual state of potential war, just as neighboring hunter-gatherer bands did twenty thousand years ago.

If the time has come when we must devise a different method of settling our disputes, it can be done only with the cooperation of the world's governments, for it is the absolute independence of national governments that makes war possible. Unfortunately, mistrust reigns everywhere, and nations seldom allow even the least of their interests to be decided by a collection of foreigners.

The nationalists are right to worry about what a powerful United Nations might mean. The United Nations was created to end war—"not to bring mankind to Heaven but to save it from Hell," in Dag Hammarskjold's words. The UN's founders knew that to guarantee each country's safety from attack by its neighbors, to make decisions on international disputes, and *to enforce them*, it would need powerful armed forces under its own command—and indeed the UN Charter makes provisions for just such a force.

A Little Bit of Principle, a Lot of Power

> Justice without force is useless.
>
> Blaise Pascal[3]

This is the real reason why the United Nations has never worked as designed: a truly effective UN would have the power to coerce national governments, so naturally governments everywhere refuse to allow it to come into being. They know what they must do to end international war—have known it since 1945 at the latest—but they are not yet willing to do it. The possibility of their own interests being damaged somewhere down the line by the decisions of a United Nations grown too mighty to resist is so worrisome that they prefer to go on living with the risk of war.

The present United Nations is certainly no place for idealists, but they would feel even more uncomfortable in a United Nations that actually worked. It would remain what it has always been—an association of poachers turned gamekeepers, not an assembly of saints—and it would not make its decisions according to some impartial standard of justice. There is no impartial concept of justice to which all of mankind would subscribe. In any case, "mankind" does not make decisions at the United Nations: governments do, with their own national interests to protect. As now, they would reach their decisions by an intensely political process, kept within the boundaries of reason only by the shared recognition that they must never damage the interests of any powerful member or group of members so badly as to destroy the fundamental consensus keeping war at bay.

We should not be shocked by this. National politics everywhere operates with the same combination: a little bit of principle, a lot of power, and a final constraint on the ruthless exercise of that power based on the need to avoid civil war and preserve the consensus on which the nation is founded. At the national level we consent to the impositions and inconveniences of a distant and unwieldy government because, in the final analysis, the benefits outweigh the costs: it gives us civil peace, protection from the rival ambitions of other national communities, and a framework for large-scale cooperation in pursuing whatever goals we set ourselves as a society.

The same arguments ought to have equal weight in favor of an international authority, but in no major country in the world is there widespread popular support for surrendering sovereignty to the United Nations. Most people are reluctant to accept that war and national sovereignty are indissolubly linked, and that to be rid of one they must give up much of the other. The vast majority of individuals believe strongly that their own nation should have complete independence.

Interestingly, this belief runs less strong within governments than among the people they govern. The United Nations was not founded by popular demand; it was created by governments who were alarmed by the path they were on and unable to ignore the grim realities of the situation. If they didn't have to worry how their own people would respond, the foreign policy professionals in almost every country would make the minimum concessions necessary to create a functioning world authority. The more reflective military professionals would concur, for the same reasons.

The obstacle is "the people": the enormous domestic resistance to any surrender of independence. It is also the politicians, for even if they understand the realities of the situation themselves (and many do not, as their backgrounds are usually in domestic issues), politicians cannot afford to get too far ahead of the people they lead. Nevertheless, progress has been made.

> We must get the modern national state before it gets us.
>
> Dwight MacDonald, 1945[4]

If the abolition of great-power war and the establishment of international law is a hundred-year project, then we are running somewhat behind schedule. But we have made substantial progress. World War III has not happened, and that is thanks, at least in part, to the United Nations giving the great powers a means to back away from their most dangerous confrontations without losing face. The UN Charter's ban on changing borders by force has not stopped all border wars, but not a single forcible redrawing of any country's boundaries has gained broad international recognition (including the Russian Seizures of the Crimea and Donbass from Ukraine). Wars between middle-sized powers—Arab-Israeli wars and Indo-Pakistani wars, mostly—seldom last more than a month because UN offers of ceasefires and peacekeeping troops provide a quick way out for the losing side.

There have also been spectacular failures, like the eight-year war between Iraq and Iran in the 1980s, which was deliberately prolonged by American and Russian aid to Saddam Hussein in the hope that he would destroy the revolutionary Islamic regime in Iran. Great-power moves like the Soviet invasion of Afghanistan in 1979 and the US invasion of Iraq in 2003 were illegal, but could not be dealt with by the UN because of the veto system. Most of the conflict deaths over the past thirty years have been the victims of civil wars (mainly in Africa) in which the UN has had no mandate to interfere.

USSR premier Alexei Kosygin greets Saddam Hussein on April 14, 1975

Viewed from a low orbit, the glass is at least half full. The survival of the UN as a permanent, all-inclusive forum whose member states are committed to avoiding or preventing war—and sometimes succeed—has already created a context new to history.

A Final Act of Redefinition

In a rapidly heating world, though, horrendous choices may be necessary. Geo-engineering techniques to slow the rise in temperatures, vital to those great powers closest to the equator, might seem less of a priority to those in the temperate zone who can afford to wait—and such a difference of opinion could spark the kind of great-power war that seems unthinkable at present.

The growth of relatively cheap but effective weapons systems (drones, robots, etc.) that can operate in swarms is leveling the playing field in ways that make big, rich powers vulnerable to crippling, anonymous attacks by small, poor ones (one recent example being the drone attack on Saudi Arabia's oil

Swarm of surveillance drones flying in formation, 2017

production in 2019). The list of potential technological and strategic surprises is long: the "unknown unknowns" will always be with us.

We are in the midst of a transformation, enabled by mass communications technology, in which human beings are reclaiming their ancient egalitarian heritage. It is not clear why becoming more democratic should make people more peaceful—egalitarian hunter-gatherers were not exactly peaceful, as we have seen—but it seems to have that effect nevertheless. Democratic countries fight wars, but they almost never fight each other. We will have to go on tweaking the institutions, or else our more egalitarian, more connected world could still be toppled back into war, but there is hope. A slow yet perceptible revolution in human consciousness is underway.

We have always run our affairs on the assumption that there is a special category of people whom we regard as full human beings, with rights and duties about equal to our own, and whom we must not kill even when we quarrel. Over the past ten thousand years we have widened this category from the original hunting-and-gathering band to embrace larger and larger groups. First it was the tribe of a few thousand people bound together by kinship and ritual ties; then the state, whose members recognize shared interests with millions of other people they don't know and will never meet; and now, finally, the entire human race.

There was nothing idealistic about those previous revisions. They happened because they advanced people's material interests and ensured their survival. The same is true for this final act of redefinition: we have reached a point where our moral imagination must expand again to include the whole of humankind, or we will perish. The shift in cultural perspective and the creation of political institutions reflecting the new perspective will take a very long time. It is hard to believe we are even halfway to our goal yet.

As for the argument that there will never be universal brotherhood among the nations: it isn't necessary. It can hardly be said to exist within any nation, so why would it flourish between them? What does exist, and must now be extended beyond all borders, is a mutual recognition that we are all better off when we respect one another's rights and accept arbitration by a higher authority, instead of killing one another when our rights or interests come into conflict. In any given year, there is only a small danger that another world war might begin and put an end to human civilization. Cumulatively, though, given how long the process of change will take, the danger is extreme. But it's no reason to stop trying.

> However deficient in many ways the United Nations may be, I think it's an absolutely essential organization. There is no way in which this effort cannot be made—it has to be made—knowing perfectly well that you're pushing an enormous boulder up a very steep hill. There will be slips and it will come back on you from time to time, but you have to go on pushing. Because if you don't do that, you simply give in to the notion that you're going to go into a global war again at some point, this time with nuclear weapons.
>
> Brian Urquhart

Our task over the next few generations is to transform the present world of independent states into some sort of genuine international community. If we succeed in creating that community, however quarrelsome, discontented, and full of injustice it will be, then we shall effectively have abolished the ancient institution of warfare. Good riddance.

Coda

I am writing this in late March of 2022, while the war begun by the Russian invasion of Ukraine is still raging and before the outcome is clear. The expectation of a swift Russian military victory followed by a long Ukrainian guerilla war against Russian occupation has already been confounded by the remarkably poor performance of the Russian army and the equally unforeseen dedication and competence of the defending Ukrainian forces. The full range of possibilities remains open at this point, from an eventual triumph of Russian numbers and firepower in the conventional war (followed by the inevitable guerrilla war) to the slow collapse of a demoralized and stalemated Russian army in Ukraine. A negotiated peace is imaginable, or even the use of a low-yield Russian nuclear weapon to demonstrate that Russian "patience" is running out (hinted at although never explicitly stated by President Putin). Yet despite my ignorance of the future, some things are fairly predictable.

First, this will not be one of those events that allegedly "changed the world forever" (a phrase that is banned in all the better journalism schools) unless we somehow contrive to get a full-on nuclear war out of it. That still seems very unlikely, because the United States and its nuclear-armed allies, Britain and France, are hyper-aware that direct fighting between them and Russia would constitute that genuine great-power war, with nuclear-armed participants on both sides, that has been avoided for almost eighty years now. Wars with a great power only on one side are commonplace and carry no such risk. In this case, Putin's attack on Ukraine will mainly serve to mark a decisive step in Russia's gradual descent from full great-power status, rather as the bungled Anglo-French attack on Egypt in 1956 did for those two former imperial powers.

As in almost every war, a few new pieces of military technology have been used in Ukraine for the first time, but no change of great importance has been revealed. The conduct of military operations would hold few surprises for veterans of any conventional war of the past fifty years, and the scale of casualties, like the size of the armies involved, remains several orders of magnitude less than that of the world wars of the early twentieth century. "Cyberwar," once again, has failed to deliver decisive or even moderately impressive results.

The one genuinely new aspect of the 2022 war was the scale and comprehensiveness of the sanctions that were imposed on Russia by Western countries. Sanctions have long been the default instrument of countries that disapprove of another country's actions but are not willing to go to war over them. They were therefore ideal for direct or proxy confrontations involving nuclear powers, precisely because they were essentially mere gestures that almost never force the target of the sanctions to change its ways. However, the brazen effrontery of the Russian invasion of Ukraine, with no plausible pretext or provocation, produced an unexpectedly united front among Western countries for sanctions so extreme that they seriously threatened the economic stability of the Russian Federation.

What is driving this reaction is not really a fear that Russia is going to conquer other parts of Europe if it is not stopped now. Russia lacks the financial and military resources to do anything of the sort. It is a belated realization that the largely successful post-1945 ban on changing borders by military force is at risk of disappearing.

The last time the ban was successfully enforced was in the first Gulf War in 1990–91, when an American-led, United Nations-authorized multinational army liberated Kuwait and put the Iraqi border back where it belonged. President George W. Bush gravely undermined that rule by invading Iraq on false pretenses and without UN authorization in 2003, but at least he stopped at regime change and did not change the country's borders. Vladimir Putin has already illegally changed Ukraine's borders once by force in 2014, and there were credible fears that he intended to abolish them entirely and incorporate the entire country into the Russian Federation this time. To let that stand would be to abandon the experiment of 1945 and accept a return to the lawless past where wars of conquest were perfectly acceptable if you won.

There are those who believe that the international rule of law was never a realistic possibility. Some of those people manage to believe that a lawless world equipped with nuclear weapons and other weapons of mass destruction nevertheless has a long-term future, while others simply accept that we are doomed by our very nature. These are matters of belief, and I do not seek to convince them otherwise. However, the international system constructed after the Second World War, and still dominant today, is based on the hope that rational self-interest will lead most people and states to support the rule of law, and that human culture is malleable enough to abandon even institutions as deeply rooted as war if they no longer serve people's interests. We shall find out which is true in due course.

Notes

Foreword

1. Robyn Dixon, "Drones owned the battlefield in Nagorno-Karabakh—and showed future of warfare," *The Washington Post*, November 11, 2020.

Chapter 1

1. J. Morgan, *The Life and Adventures of William Buckley: Thirty-Two Years A Wanderer Amongst the Aborigines* (Canberra: Australian National University Press, 1979 [1852]), 49–51.

2. W. L. Warner, "Murngin Warfare," *Oceania* I (1931): 457–94.

3. N. A. Chagnon, *Studying the Yanomamo* (New York: Holt, Rinehart and Winston, 1974), 157–61; N. A. Chagnon, *Yanomamo*, 4th edition (New York: Harcourt and Brace: Jovanovich College Publishers, 1994), 205.

4. E. S. Burch Jr., "Eskimo Warfare in Northwest Alaska," *Anthropological Papers of the University of Alaska* 16, no. 2 (1974): 1–14.

5. Richard Wrangham and Dale Peterson, *Demonic Males: Apes and the Origins of Human Violence* (Boston: Houghton Mifflin, 1996), 17.

6. Stephen A. LeBlanc and Katherine E. *Register*, Constant Battles: The Myth of the Noble, Peaceful Savage (New York: St. Martin's Press, 2003), 81–85.

7. Ibid., 94–97.

8. Wrangham and Peterson, op. cit., 65.

9. Harold Schneider, *Livestock and Equality in East Africa*: *The Economic Basis for Social Structure* (Bloomington and London: Indiana University Press, 1979), 210.

10. Bruce Knauft, "Violence and Sociality in Human Evolution," *Current Anthropology* 32, no. 4 (Aug.–Oct. 1991): 391–428.

11. Christopher Boehm, *Hierarchy in the Forest* (Boston: Harvard University Press, 2001).

12. Richard B. Lee, *The !Kung San: Men, Women and Work in a Foraging Society* (Cambridge: Cambridge University Press, 1979).

Chapter 2

1. John Ellis, *The Sharp End of War* (North Pomfret, VT: David and Charles, 1980), 162–64; Richard Holmes, *Acts of War: The Behaviour of Men in Battle* (London, Random House, 2003).

2. M. Lindsay, *So Few Got Through* (London: Arrow, 1955), 249.

3. Samuel P. Huntington, *The Soldier and the State* (New York: Vintage, 1964), 79.

4. S. Bagnall, *The Attack,* (London: Hamish Hamilton, 1947), 21

5. S. A. Stouffer et al., *The American Soldier*, vol. II (Princeton, NJ: Princeton University Press, 1949), 202.

6. Lt. Col. J. W. Appel and Capt. G. W. Beebe, "Preventive Psychiatry: An Epidemiological Approach," *Journal of the American Medical Association* 131 (1946): 1470.

7. Bagnall, op. cit., 160.

8. Appel and Beebe, op. cit.

9. Col. S. L. A. Marshall, *Men Against Fire* (New York: William Morrow and Co., 1947), 149–50.

10. Martin Middlebrook, *The Battle of Hamburg* (London: Allen Lane, 1980), 244.

11. "Gunner—Unmanned Aerial Systems," The British Army, army.mod.uk.

12. See airwars.org. The Bureau of Investigative Journalism gives much more conservative estimates of 14,040 "minimum confirmed strikes" by US armed drones and 8,858–16,901 "total killed," of whom only 910–2,200 were civilians. Airwars also counts unannounced American drone strikes (including those in Pakistan), and strikes by Russian drones in Syria; Turkish drones in Iraq, Syria, and Libya; Saudi Arabian and UAE drones in Yemen; and so on.

13. "Distinguished Warfare Medal cancelled," American Legion, legion.org.

14. Patrick Wintour, "RAF urged to recruit video game players to operate Reaper drones," *The Guardian*, December 9, 2016.

15. D. Wallace and J. Costello, "Eye in the sky: Understanding the mental health of unmanned aerial vehicle operators," *Journal of Military and Veteran's Health* 28, no. 3 (October 2020).

16. Eyal Press, "The Wounds of the Drone Warrior," *New York Times Magazine*, June 13, 2018.

17. Sky News interview, November 8, 2020.

18. For a full discussion of the legal issues involved in regulating the development and use of autonomous weapons, see Frank Pasquale, *New Laws of Robotics: Defending Human Expertise in the Age of AI* (Boston: Harvard University Press, 2020).

Chapter 3

1. Robert L. O'Connell, *Ride of the Second Horseman: The Growth and Death of War* (Oxford: Oxford University Press, 1995), 64–66; John Keegan, *A History of Warfare* (New York: Vintage, 1994), 124–26.

2. O'Connell, op. cit., 68–76.

3. Homer, *Iliad*, tr. Richard Lattimore (Chicago: University of Chicago Press, 1951), 65–84.

4. Samuel Noah Kramer, *History Begins at Sumer* (Philadelphia: University of Pennsylvania Press, 1981), 30–32.

5. O'Connell, op. cit., 77–83; Keegan, op. cit., 156–57.

6. Keegan, op. cit., 181.

7. Ibid., 166.

8. O'Connell, op. cit., 122, 165–66; Keegan, op. cit., 168.

Chapter 4

1. H. W. F. Saggs, *The Might That Was Assyria* (London: Sidgwick & Jackson,1984), 197.

2. Robert L. O'Connell, *Ride of the Second Horseman: The Growth and Death of War* (Oxford: Oxford University Press, 1995), 145–58.

3. Virgil, *The Aeneid*, tr. W. F. Jackson Knight (London: Penguin Books, 1968), 62–65.

4. The eyewitness account of Polybius itself is lost, but this account by Appian is directly based on it. Susan Rowen, *Rome in Africa* (London: Evans Brothers, 1969), 32–33.

5. Graham Webster, *The Roman Imperial Army* (London: Adam Charles Black, 1969), 221.

6. Herodotus, describing the battle of Marathon, in *The Histories*, tr. Aubrey de Selincourt (London: Penguin, 1954,) 428–29.

7. Aeschylus, *The Persians*, lines 355 ff. For dramatic purposes, Aeschylus was describing the battle from the Persian side.

8. Thucydides, *History of the Peloponnesian Wars* (London: Penguin, 1952), 523–24.

9. Keith Hopkins, *Conquerors and Slaves, Sociological Studies in Roman History*, vol. 1 (Cambridge: At the University Press, 1978), 33.

10. Ibid., 28.

11. Edward N. Luttwak, *The Grand Strategy of the Roman Empire from the First Century AD to the Third Century AD* (Baltimore: Johns Hopkins Press, 1976), 15, 189.

Chapter 5

1. Charles C. Oman, *The Art of War in the Sixteenth Century* (London: Methuen, 1937), 237–38.

2. Ibid., 240.

3. Douglas E. Streusand, *Islamic Gunpowder Empires: Ottomans, Safavids, and Mughals* (Philadelphia: Westview Press, 2011), 83.

4. Andre Corvisier, *Armies and Societies in Europe 1494–1789* (Bloomington, Indiana: University of Indiana Press, 1979), 28.

5. J. J. Saunders, *The History of the Mongol Conquests* (London: Routledge and Kegan Paul, 1971), 197–98.

6. C. V. Wedgwood, *The Thirty Years' War* (London: Jonathan Cape, 1956), 288–89.

7. J. F. Puysegur, *L'art de la guerre par principes et par règles* (Paris, 1748), i.

8. Edward Mead Earle, ed., *Makers of Modern Strategy* (New York: Atheneum, 1966), 56.

9. Hew Strachan, *European Armies and the Conduct of War* (London: George Allen and Unwin, 1983), 8.

10. Laurence Sterne, *A Sentimental Journey through France and Italy* (Oxford: Basil Blackwell, 1927), 85.

11. Christopher Duffy, *The Army of Frederick the Great* (London: David and Charles, 1974), 62.

12. Strachan, op. cit., 9.

13. Martin van Crefeld, *Supplying War: Logistics from Wallenstein to Patton* (Cambridge: Cambridge University Press, 1977), 38.

14. Maurice, Comte de Saxe, *Les Rêveries, ou Mémoires sur l'Art de la Guerre* (Paris: Jean Drieux, 1757), 77.

15. Alexander Koch et al., "Earth system impacts of the European arrival and Great Dying in the Americas after 1492," *Quaternary Science Reviews* 207 (2019): 13–36.

Chapter 6

1. Edward Gibbon, *The Decline and Fall of the Roman Empire* (New York: The Modern Library, 1932).

2. Maj. Gen. J. F. C. Fuller, *The Conduct of War, 1789–1961* (London: Eyre and Spottiswoode, 1961), 32.

3. R. D. Challener, *The French Theory of the Nation in Arms, 1866–1939* (New York: Russell and Russell, 1965), 3; Alfred Vagts, *A History of Militarism*, rev. ed. (New York: Meridian, 1959), 108–11.

4. Vagts, op. cit., 114; Karl von Clausewitz, *On War*, eds. and trs. Michael Howard and Peter Paret (Princeton, New Jersey: Princeton University Press, 1976).

5. Vagts, op.cit., 126–37; John Gooch, *Armies in Europe* (London: Routledge and Kegan Paul, 1980), 39.

6. David Mitch, "Education and Skill of the British Labour Force," *The Cambridge Economic History of Modern Britain, Vol. I: Industrialisation, 1700–1860*, eds. Roderick Floud and Paul Johnson (Cambridge: Cambridge University Press, 2004), 344.

7. Eltjo Buringh and Jan Luiten van Zanden, "Charting the 'Rise of the West' Manuscripts and Printed Books in Europe, A Long-Term Perspective from the Sixth through Eighteenth Centuries," *The Journal of Economic History* 69, no. 2 (2009): 409–45.

8. Anthony Brett-James, *Eyewitness Accounts of Napoleon's Defeat in Russia* (London: Macmillan, 1967), 127.

9. Christopher Duffy, *Borodino and the War of 1812* (London: Seeley Service, 1972), 135.

10. David Chandler, *The Campaigns of Napoleon* (New York: Macmillan, 1966), 668; Gooch, op. cit., 39–41.

11. Vagts, op. cit., 143–44.

12. Ibid., 140.

13. Edward Meade Earle, ed., *Makers of Modern Strategy* (New York: Atheneum, 1966), 57.

14. Karl von Clausewitz, *On War*, tr. Col. J. J. Graham (London: Trubner, 1873), i, 4.

15. Paddy Griffith, *Battle Tactics of the Civil War* (New Haven, CT: Yale University Press, 1987), 144–50.

16. Frank E. Vandiver, *Mighty Stonewall* (New York: McGraw-Hill, 1957), 366.

17. Col. Theodore Lyman, *Meade's Headquarters, 1863–1865* (Boston: Massachusetts Historical Society, 1922), 101, 224.

18. Mark Grimsley, "Surviving Military Revolution: The US Civil War," *The Dynamics of Military Revolution, 1300–2050*, eds. Knox and Williamson Murray (Cambridge: Cambridge University Press, 2001), 84.

19. Frederick Henry Dyer, *A Compendium of The War of the Rebellion* (New York: T. Yoseloff, 1959).

20. *Personal Memoirs of General W. T. Sherman* (Bloomington, Indiana: Indiana University Press, 1957), ii, 111.

Chapter 7

1. I. S. Bloch, *The War of the Future in Its Technical, Economic and Political Relations*, tr. W. T. Stead (*Is War Impossible?*, 1899).

2. Jacques d'Arnoux, "Paroles d'un revenant," *L'atmosphere du Champ de Bataille*, ed. Lieut.-Col. J. Armengaud (Paris: Lavauzelle, 1940), 118–19.

3. J. E. C. Fuller, *The Second World War, 1939–1945: A Strategic and Tactical History* (New York: Duell, Sloan and Pearce, 1949), 140.

4. Ibid., 170; Keegan, op. cit., 309.

5. Henry Williamson, *The Wet Flanders Plain* (London: Beaumont Press), 14–16. Williamson was nineteen years old during the Battle of the Somme.

6. Arthur Bryant, *Unfinished Victory* (London: Macmillan, 1940), 8.

7. Aaron Norman, *The Great Air War* (New York: Macmillan, 1968), 353.

8. Bryan Perret, *A History of Blitzkrieg* (London: Robert Hale, 1983), 21.

9. Jonathan B. A. Bailey, "The Birth of Modern Warfare," Knox and Murray, op. cit., 142–45.

10. Sir William Robertson, *Soldiers and Statesmen* (London: Cassell, 1926), i, 313.

11. Theodore Ropp, *War in the Modern World*, rev. ed. (New York: Collier, 1962), 321, 344.

12. Guy Sajer, *The Forgotten Soldier* (London: Sphere, 1977), 228–30.

13. Giulio Douhet, *The Command of the Air* (London: Faber & Faber, 1943), 18–19.

14. Max Hastings, *Bomber Command* (London: Pan Books, 1979), 129.

15. Martin Middlebrook, *The Battle of Hamburg* (London: Allen Lane, 1980), 264–67.

16. Craven and Cate, *US Army Air Forces*, vol. 5 (Chicago: University of Chicago Press, 1948), 615–17.

17. H. H. Arnold, *Report to the Secretary of War; 12 November 1945* (Washington, DC: Government Printing Office, 1945), 35.

18. Leonard Bickel, *The Story of Uranium: The Deadly Element* (London: Macmillan, 1979), 78–79, 198–99, 274–76.

Chapter 8

1. Bernard Brodie, ed., *The Absolute Weapon: Atomic Power and World Order* (New York: Harcourt Brace, 1946), 76.

2. Fred Kaplan, *The Wizards of Armageddon* (New York: Simon & Schuster, 1983), 26–32.

3. Ibid.

4. Gregg Herken, *Counsels of War* (New York: Knopf, 1985), 306.

5. Kaplan, op. cit., 133–34.

6. Herken, op. cit., 116.

7. Gerard C. Smith, *Doubletalk: The Story of the First Strategic Arms Limitation Talks* (Garden City, NY: Doubleday, 1980), 10–11.

8. Desmond Ball, "Targeting for Strategic Deterrence," *Adelphi Papers*, no. 185 (1983): 40.

9. *New York Times*, May 12, 1968.

10. Herken, op. cit., 143–45; Ball, op. cit., 10.

11. Kaplan, op. cit., 242–43, 272–73, 278–80; Herken, op. cit., 51, 145; Ball, op. cit., 10–11.

12. Robert F. Kennedy, *Thirteen Days: A Memoir of the Cuban Missile Crisis* (New York: Norton, 1968), 156.

13. "The Cuban Missile Crisis, 1962: A Political Perspective After Forty Years," The National Security Archive of George Washington University, gwu.edu.

14. McGeorge Bundy et al., "The President's Choice; Star Wars or Arms Control," *Foreign Affairs* 63, no. 2 (Winter 1984–85): 271.

15. Carl Sagan, "Nuclear War and Climatic Catastrophe: Some Policy Implications," *Foreign Affairs* (Winter 1983–84): 285.

16. R. P. Turco et al., "Nuclear Winter: Global Consequences of Multiple Nuclear Explosions," *Science* 222 (1983): 1283–97; R.P. Turco et al., "The Climatic Effects of Nuclear War," *Scientific American* 251, no. 2 (1984): 33–43.

17. Paul R. Ehrlich et al., "The Long-Term Biological Consequences of Nuclear War," *Science* 222, no. 4630 (1983): 1293–1300.

18. Sagan, op. cit., 276; Turco et al., op. cit., 38.

19. *Science* 247 (1990): 166–76.

Chapter 9

1. Kaufmann's 1955 essays were very influential in shaping the United States army's thinking on the possibility of restricting war in Europe to conventional weapons. Fred Kaplan, *The Wizards of Armageddon* (New York: Knopf, 1984), 197–200.

2. Karl von Clausewitz, *On War* (New York: The Modern Library, 1943).

3. W. Baring Pemberton, *Lord Palmerston* (London: Collins, 1954), 220–21.

4. Stanley Karnow, *Vietnam: A History* (New York: Viking, 1983), 312.

5. Walter Laqueur, *Guerilla* (London: Weidenfeld and Nicholson, 1977), 40.

6. Christon I. Archer et al., *World History of Warfare* (London: Cassell, 2003), 558.

7. Robert Moss, *Urban Guerillas* (London: Temple Smith, 1972), 198.

8. Sarah Ewing, "The IoS Interview," *Independent on Sunday*, September 8, 2002.

Chapter 10

1. Natalie Angier, "No Time for Bullies: Baboons Retool Their Culture," *The New York Times*, April 13, 2004.

2. "India's Actions in Kashmir Risk Nuclear War," *The Guardian*, September 28, 2019.

3. Blaise Pascal, *Pensées*, chapter 3, section 285 (1660), *Oeuvres completes* (Gallimard, 1969), 1160.

4. Dwight MacDonald, *Politics* magazine, August 1945.

Image Credits

p. 7 Cover of *Yanomamö* by Napoleon A. Chagnon. Pub. Holt, Rinehart, Winston, 2nd ed., 1977.

p. 9 Jane Goodall, ca 1965. Contributor: Everett Collection Historical / Alamy Stock Photo.

p. 20 Bushmen in Namibia. Creative Commons. © Archiv Dr. Rüdiger Wenzel.

p. 23 *Vietnam. . . . A* Marine *walking point for his unit during Operation Macon moves slowly, cautious of enemy pitfalls.* U.S. National Archives and Records Administration, 1966. Public Domain.

p. 27 Red Army shoulder marks, c. 1943. Public Domain.

p. 30 Korean War, one infantryman comforts another while a third fills out body tags, Aug. 25, 1950, Sfc. Al Chang, US Army Korea Medical Center. Public Domain.

p. 37 A new recruit responds to drill instructors, Marine Corps Recruitment Depot, San Diego. marines.mil. Public Domain.

p. 41 Gabreski in the cockpit of his P47 Thunderbolt after his 28th kill (and 5 days before his capture). U.S. National Archives and Records Administration. Public Domain.

p. 49 David Wreckham on an anti-killer robot leafletting drive outside Parliament in April. Photograph: Oli Scarff/Getty Images.

p. 59 Stele of Vultures, c. 2450 BC, Dept of Mesopotamian Antiquities, Louvre Museum, France, photo Commons: by Eric Gaba, July 5.

p. 64 Scythians shooting with composite bows, Kerch, Crimea, 4th century BCE, Louvre Museum, photo Commons: PHGcom, 2007.

p. 67 Possible chariot on the Bronocile pot, Poland, c. 3500 BCE, Archaeological Museum, Krakow, Commons, user Silar.

p. 74 Siege tower on Assyrian bas-relief, NW Palace of Nimrud, c. 865-860 BCE, British Museum, Commons, user: capillon, June 12, 2008.

p. 77 Hoplites fighting, design on an urn before 5th century BCE, Athens Archaeological Museum. Public Domain.

p. 80 Carthaginian war elephants engage Roman infantry at the Battle of Zama, Henri-Paul Motte. *Das Wissen des 20. Jahrhunderts*, Bildungslexikon, Rheda, 1931. Public Domain.

p. 81 Artist's rendition of the trireme commanded by Pytheas (c. 300 BCE). From *The Romance of Early British Life*, by G. F. Scott Elliot, 1909 illustration by John F. Campbell. Public Domain.

p. 89 4th-century miniature from William of Tyre's *Histoire d'Outremer* of a battle during the Second Crusade, National Library of France, Department of Manuscripts, French. Public Domain.

p. 92 Infantry on the march, wood engraving after a relief on the tomb of King Francis I (died in 1547). INTERFOTO/History/Alamy Stock Photo.

p. 96 First illustration of Fire Lance, 10th century, Dunhuang. A detail from an illustration of Sakyamuni's temptation by Mara. Public Domain.

p. 99 Tilly's entry into the destroyed city of Magdeburg on May 25, from p. 245 of *Deutschlands letztere drei Jahrhunderte, oder: des deutschen Volkes Gedenk-Buch an seiner Väter Schicksale und Leiden seit drei Jahrhunderten, etc.* By Franz Lubojatzky, 1858. Public Domain.

p. 103 Musket Drill: *L'Art Militaire pour l'Infanterie*, de Johann Jacobi von Wallhausen, Leewarden, Claude Fontaine, 1630. Public Domain.

p. 105 The Storming of the Schellenberg at Donauwörth. Detail of tapestry by Judocus de Vos c. 18th century, Blenheim Palace. Wikimedia Commons. Public Domain Art.

p. 113 Napoleon Bonaparte (1769–1821) as Emperor Napoleon 1 of France reviewing the Grenadiers of the Imperial Guard on 1 June 1811 in Paris, France. An engraving by Augustin Burdet from an original painting by Auguste Raffet. (Photo by Hulton Archive/Getty Images.)

p. 119 The Withdrawal of the Grand Army from Russia, by Johann Adam Klein. AKG images: ID AKG108396.

p. 121 Certificate of the award of the Iron Cross 2nd class for Edgar Wintrath, awarded to him on October 2, 1918. Wikimedia Commons. Public Domain.

p. 126 Soldiers in the trenches before battle, Petersburg, Virginia, America, 1865. Public Domain.

p. 135 Female munitions workers operating lathes in a British shell factory. Note the improvised wooden machinery guards used in the works. © Imperial War Museum Q 54648.

p. 137 Top: WWI poster—"It is far better to face the bullets than to be killed at home by a bomb. Join the army at once & help to stop an air raid. God save the King." 1915. United States Library of Congress's Prints and Photographs division ID cph.3g10972. Public Domain. Bottom: The wreck of Zeppelin L33 at Little Wigborough, Essex. September, 1916. Essex Record Office. Creative Commons: Official Record of the Great War, H. D. Girdwood (India Office, 1921).

p. 139 The first official photograph taken of a tank going into action, at the Battle of Flers-Courcelette. 15 September, 1916. Q 2488 ©Imperial War Museum.

p. 141 German boy soldiers WWI. Photograph probably taken in 1917. Public Domain.

p. 145 *Springfield Union* Headline: "Germany's long-delayed offensive against Russia opens on 165-mile front." Public Domain.

p. 150 Oblique aerial view of ruined residential and commercial buildings south of the Eilbektal Park (seen at upper right) in the Eilbek district of Hamburg, Germany. These were among the 16,000 multistoried apartment buildings destroyed by the firestorm that developed during the raid by Bomber Command on the night of 27/28 July, 1943 (Operation GOMORRAH). By Dowd J (Fg Off), Royal Air Force official photographer. Wikimedia Commons. IWM Non-Commercial License photo CL 3400. Public Domain.

p. 154 Firestorm cloud over Hiroshima, near local noon. August 6, 1945. US Military. Public Domain.

p. 155 General Buck Turgidson (George C. Scott) demonstrating a B-52 flying low enough to fry chickens in a barnyard in *Dr. Strangelove* trailer from 40th Anniversary Special Edition DVD, 2004, from *Dr. Strangelove or: How I Learned to Stop Worrying and Love the Bomb* by Stanley Kubrick, 1964. Wikimedia Commons. Public Domain.

p. 165 Theatrical release poster for *Duck and Cover* film, by Anthony Rizzo, 1952. Wikimedia Commons. Public Domain.

p. 166 Low-altitude reconnaissance photograph showing a nuclear warhead bunker under construction, prefabrication materials, and construction personnel at site number 1 in San Cristobal, Cuba. United States. Department of Defense. Department of Defense Cuban Missile Crisis Briefing Materials. John F. Kennedy Presidential Library and Museum, Boston. 23 October 1962. Accession No. PX66-20:20. Public Domain.

p. 170 A "personnel reliability program" examines details of each crew member's personal life to make sure they are mentally fit to carry out the great responsibility of controlling nuclear weapons. U.S. Air Force photo. VIRIN: 090108-F-1234P-010.JPG. https://www.nationalmuseum.af.mil/Upcoming/Photos/igphoto/2000642472/ Public Domain.

p. 171 Strategic Defense Initiative logo. United States Missile Defense Agency, US Federal Government. Wikimedia Commons. Public Domain.

p. 173 Soviet premier Mikhail Gorbachev shaking hands with US president Ronald Reagan in the 1980s. Everett Collection Inc/Alamy Stock Photo.

p. 178 Albert Einstein portrait, 1945. ALAMY. Alamy ID: P89CC5.

p. 187 British troops taking part in NATO's Exercise Lionheart in Germany 1984. Courtesy of the National Army Museum, London.

p. 188 An Israeli tank crossing the Suez Canal during the Arab-Israeli War. From the booklet President Nixon and the Role of Intelligence in the 1973 Arab-Israeli War. 1 October, 1973. Wikimedia Commons. Central Intelligence Agency. Public Domain.

Index

NOTE: Page references in *italics* refer to figures and photos. Page references follow by "n" refer to footnotes.

E

Eannatum, 59–60
Ecnomus, 84
Egypt, 69, 70, 163, 188–89, 194, 240
Ehrlich, Paul R., 176
Einstein, Albert, 178, *178*
Eisenhower, Dwight, 161
Ellsberg, Daniel, 164–65
end of war, 215–38
  for animals, 215–17
  cooperation or else, 223–26
  post–Cold War "peace," 172–73, 217–19
  redefinitions, 235–38
  threats to, 219–23
  United Nations and, 230–35
England. *See* Great Britain
Eritrea, 200
Euskadi ta Askatasuna (ETA), 205

F

Falklands war (1982), 190
Ferrero, Guglielmo, 182
Fitzgerald, F. Scott, 186
Flers-Courcelette, battle of (1916), *139*
Fog of War (documentary), 156, 168
Fontenoy, battle of (1745), 102
France
  cyclic pattern of world wars and, 181–83
  global politics and, 239–40
  limited war era, 91–93, 97–98, 102, *103*, 104, 106–7
  mass warfare era, 112–15, 116, 118–21, 123
  nuclear era, 162–63
  World War I, 130–31, 132, 133, 134–36, 140
  World War I aftermath, 142
  World War II, 144
  World War II aftermath, 225–26
François, Charles, 119
Frederick the Great, 105
Fussell, Paul, 27

G

Gabreski, "Gabby," *41*
Geneva Conventions (1949), 228
Germany
  classical war era, 87–88
  cyclic pattern of world wars and, 181–83
  guerrilla warfare, 197, 205
  limited war era, 92–93, 98–100, 101
  nuclear era, 152, 162, 184–87, *187*
  terrorists and, 211
  war crimes, 227–28
  World War I, 130–31, 134–41, *137*, *141*
  World War I aftermath, 142–43
  World War II, 39–40, 42–43, 143–51, *145*, 227–28
Gibbon, Edward, 111, 112
Gilgamesh (King), 60–61
Goodall, Jane, 9–11, *9*
Gorbachev, Mikhail, 172–73, *173*
Great Britain
  combat training, 43, 44, 45, 46–47, *49*
  global politics, 230–31, 239–40
  limited war era, 91, 102, 107, 108–9
  mass warfare era, 115–16, 118
  nuclear era, 157, 162–63, *187*
  revolution in military affairs, 189–90, *190*
  World War I, 130, 132, 133–34, *135*, 137–41, *137*
  World War I aftermath, 142
  World War II, 25–26, 33, 144, *145*, 148–49, *150*, 152, 189–90, *190*
  World War II aftermath, 225–26
Greece, 61, 69, 70, 73–74, 76–79, *77*, 81–83, *82*, 132
guerrilla warfare, 196–205
Gustavus Adolphus (King), 100–101

About the Author

GWYNNE DYER lives in London, where he works as an author, historian, and independent journalist. His television series on the history of war was nominated for an Academy Award, and his twice-weekly column on international affairs appears in 175 newspapers in 45 countries. He is currently working on a book about the science of planetary engineering and its geopolitical ramifications.

gwynnedyer.com

Also available in the Shortest History series

Trade Paperback Originals • $15.95 US | $21.00 CAN

978-1-61519-569-5

978-1-61519-814-6

978-1-61519-820-7

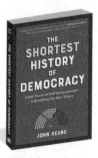

978-1-61519-896-2